A Short History
of the Vietnam War

Other Pocket Essentials by this Author:

A Short History of Europe
A Short History of Africa
A Short History of China
A Short History of Brazil
A Short History of the First World War

A SHORT HISTORY OF
THE VIETNAM WAR

GORDON KERR

POCKET ESSENTIALS

First published in 2015 by
Pocket Essentials, an imprint of
Oldcastle Books Ltd, P.O.Box 394,
Harpenden, Herts, AL5 1XJ
www.pocketessentials.com

Editor: Nick Rennison

A CIP catalogue record for this book is available from the British Library.

ISBN
978-1-84344-213-4 (Print)
978-1-84344-214-1 (epub)
978-1-84344-215-8 (Kindle)
978-1-84344-216-5 (PDF)

2 4 6 8 10 9 7 5 3 1

Typeset by Avocet Typeset, Somerton, Somerset
in 11.5pt Perpetua
Printed in Great Britain by Clays Ltd, St Ives plc

For Lindsey and Sean

'And it's one, two, three,
What are we fighting for?
Don't ask me, I don't give a damn,
Next stop is Vietnam;
And it's five, six, seven,
Open up the pearly gates,
Well there ain't no time to wonder why,
Whoopee! we're all gonna die.'

(*I Feel Like I'm Fixin' to Die Rag*, written by
Country Joe McDonald and performed by
Country Joe and the Fish)

***

A thousand years of Chinese reign.
A hundred years of French domain.
Twenty years fighting brothers each day.
A mother's fate, our fields so dead,
And rows of homes in flames so red.

(From *A Mother's Legacy*, written by
Vietnamese composer, Trinh Cong Son)

Contents

Introduction   9

Chapter 1: Two Thousand Years of Warfare   11

Chapter 2: The First Indochina War   20

Chapter 3: Keeping the Dominoes Standing:
            President Eisenhower   31

Chapter 4: Unwavering Commitment:
            President Kennedy   39

Chapter 5   Other Belligerents   44

Chapter 6: Americanising the War:
            President Johnson   48

Chapter 7: 'Peace with Honour':
            President Nixon   93

Chapter 8: The Fall of South Vietnam   139

Chapter 9: The Legacy of the Vietnam War   148

Meanings of Common Acronyms Used in the War   150

Bibliography and Filmography   152

Index   154

Introduction

The student of Vietnamese history could not be blamed for believing that country to have always been at war, blighted as its history is by invading armies and foreigners eager to hold sway over the Vietnamese people. On and off, for 2,000 years, war has raged on its soil as the Chinese, the Mongols, the French and the Americans have attempted to bend Vietnam to their will. To a greater or smaller degree, they have all failed and even the might of the United States, with its vastly superior firepower and all the technology of modern warfare, could not defeat a people fired by a passion for freedom, independence and the unification of their ancient land.

The conflict known as the Vietnam War is in reality several wars but is generally accepted to have begun in 1945 when the Viet Minh went into battle against the French colonial power. After the French had withdrawn from Indochina, following the catastrophe of the Battle of Dien Bien Phu, it fell to the Americans to try to keep communism at bay in the region. Thus did Vietnam become part of the global struggle between the two competing dogmas – capitalism and communism – that cast such a shadow over the second half of the twentieth century. Tens of thousands of Vietnamese, both North and South, Cambodians, Laotians, Australians, New Zealanders and Americans lost their lives in the ensuing war and the financial cost ran to billions of dollars. It was not a war that drew in many nations like the Second World War, but it is considered to be one of the most important conflicts of the twentieth century, affecting, as it did, the countries that fought in it, but also resonating down through the years with its impact on the domestic and foreign policy of one of the world's superpowers, the United States. It influenced not only the policies of Presidents Jimmy Carter and Ronald Reagan but its lessons were also applied to American involvement in the Gulf War in the 1990s during the presidency of George H. W. Bush.

Khang Chien Chong My (Resistance War Against America), as the Vietnamese call it, is a war that is still the subject of a great deal of controversy and the sheer volume of books published about it is testament to the fascination it holds for historians and students of war and politics. It was a conflict filled with contradictions and puzzles. Most experts cannot even agree on when it began and when it ended, for instance. And debate continues about how the United States managed to become so involved in a far-away and deeply unpopular war and how successive presidents were reluctant to walk away from Indochina, instead gradually escalating American involvement until it was almost impossible to extract themselves from it.

This book may not provide the answers to the complex questions about the conflict that have exercised brilliant minds for the decades following the fall of Saigon. Rather, it seeks to follow the story of French and American involvement and the astonishing struggle of the North Vietnamese and many South Vietnamese to make their dream of unification come to pass.

1

Two Thousand Years of Warfare

Invasion and Civil War

On 8 March 1965, 3,500 US Marines of Battalion Landing Team 3/9 waded ashore in full regalia on the sandy beaches of Da Nang in South Vietnam, their mission to provide security for the nearby air base that was thought vulnerable to attack. They were the first American combat troops to step onto Asian soil since the end of the Korean War in 1953. But they were by no means the first foreign army to set foot on Vietnamese soil.

Vietnam has one of the longest continuous histories in the world. Humans were first present there around 500,000 years ago and it boasts some of the world's earliest civilizations, such as the Hoa Binh and Bac Son cultures. At the same time as Mesopotamia was discovering agriculture it was also being practised in Southeast Asia and pottery was also being manufactured. In approximately 2879 BC, the first Vietnamese state emerged in the Red River valley in northern Vietnam when the need to work together for flood prevention, for trade and for fighting off invaders necessitated a single authority that would take responsibility for organising such things. From there in 207 BC comes the first documented historical reference to a kingdom known as Nam Viet or Nanyue. At the time, the kingdom was ruled by a Chinese general, indicating that the Chinese controlled the region and they would, in fact, remain in power there for another thousand years. But, despite having a

Chinese-style bureaucracy and using Chinese methods of rice cultivation, Nam Viet remained a separate kingdom. In 111 BC, however, Chinese Han Dynasty troops invaded and established new regions – Giao Chi in the Red River (Song Hong) delta; Curu Chan which stretched from modern-day Thanh Hoa to Ha Tinh; and Nhat Nam, stretching from modern-day Quang Binh to Hue.

During the thousand years that the northern part of Vietnam remained a Chinese province, it was dominated by the culture of its conqueror but still retained a keen hunger for independence. Unlike many other peoples under Chinese suzerainty, for example, the Vietnamese clung on to their distinctively Vietnamese culture. They maintained their totemic beliefs which were in contrast to Chinese practice, for instance. On the other hand, Confucianism, the ethical and philosophical system that supported Chinese society, pervaded the ruling class in Vietnam. In this set of beliefs, the emperor's authority was inviolable and it was believed that he ruled with the so-called 'Mandate of Heaven'; he had been bestowed the right to rule by heaven itself. This created an entire social and political hierarchy, featuring many elite Vietnamese families which seized upon Confucianism as a means of legitimising and maintaining their status in society. The majority of Vietnamese people, meanwhile, were peasants living in small villages that held on to Vietnamese traditions and practices.

Chinese domination eventually ended in 938 when a Chinese Southern Han force, sent to conquer the autonomous region of Giao Chi, was defeated by the army of the Vietnamese prefect and general, Ngo Quyen (897-944), at the naval Battle of Bach Dang River, near Ha Long Bay in northern Vietnam. During the next thousand years, Vietnam changed little. Authority was wielded by kings who worked hard to prevent any member of the elite from establishing a power base that could be used to challenge the ruler. Vietnamese society, governed by a class of Mandarin bureaucrats who endured similarly rigorous training to their Chinese counterparts, remained stable, immune to social, cultural or technological change and innovation.

There were a number of challenges to Vietnamese stability, however. The Chinese Song Dynasty, for instance, attempted to recapture the region in 1075, but its troops were repelled, as they were the following year. Subsequent decades saw more invasions. During the Vietnamese Tran Dynasty (1225-1400), there were three incursions by the all-conquering Mongols – in 1257, 1284 and 1287 – but their large armies were all defeated. Like their North Vietnamese and Viet Cong descendants some seven hundred years later, the thirteenth-century Vietnamese did this by refusing to face the Mongols in large-scale set-piece battles or in sieges, confronting them instead in locations that put the invaders at a distinct disadvantage, on terrain that would prove difficult to them. The Yuan (Mongol) fleet was decisively defeated by the Vietnamese at the 1288 Battle of Bach Dang.

The Chinese Ming Dynasty invaded and occupied Vietnam in the early 1400s, but its domination lasted for only around twenty years and once again stubborn Vietnamese resistance saw them off. The hero of the hour and one of the great figures of Vietnamese history emerged around this time. Wealthy farmer, Le Loi (r. 1428-33) waged war against the Chinese initially to restore the Tran Dynasty to the throne, but eventually, under the sobriquet 'the Pacifying King' (Binh Dinh Vuong), he took the throne. By 1427, Le Loi's revolt against Chinese rule had spread throughout Vietnam, leading the Chinese to make one last attempt to control the country, by dispatching a huge army of around 100,000 troops. The Vietnamese force they faced, however, was 350,000 strong and the Chinese were destroyed in a series of battles in 1428, reportedly losing 90,000 men – 60,000 killed and 30,000 taken prisoner. The Ming Emperor Xuande (1399-1435) had no option but to accept Vietnamese independence, freeing Le Loi to establish his own dynasty.

Le Loi next embarked on the initiative known as the 'March

to the South' with the objective of conquering the large kingdom of Champa that occupied the area of today's central and southern Vietnam. This was achieved in 1471 and was followed, during the next two and a half centuries by the conquest of further southern coastal lands. The Le/Trinh and Mac dynasties fought for control of Vietnam between 1545 and 1592 when Hanoi fell to the Trinh and the Mac ruler was executed. Civil war between the rival Trinh and Nguyen families raged between 1627 and 1672 when a truce was agreed that effectively split Vietnam in two, the Nguyen family ruling the south and the Trinh family in control of the north.

By 1701, the southern half of the country reached as far south as the Ca Mau Peninsula, on the southern tip of the modern country of Vietnam, the Mekong Delta having been captured from the Khmer Kingdom between the middle of the seventeenth and the beginning of the eighteenth century. Such expansion made it almost impossible to maintain central control, however, and, during this time, the country endured civil war and lengthy schisms.

The Arrival of the Europeans

Europeans had first visited Vietnam as far back as 166 BC when Roman merchants had made the long, perilous journey from Europe. The Venetian merchant and explorer Marco Polo visited in 1292 and Portuguese traders as well as other European merchants and missionaries arrived in the early sixteenth century. French influence in the region began with the arrival of the French Jesuit priest, Alexandre de Rhodes (1591-1660) who, having learned the Vietnamese language, created a Romanised version of its alphabet. De Rhodes worked initially in the north, but was expelled in 1630 after the ruler and his counsellors turned against Christianity. By this time Christian missionaries were being viewed as a threat to the Confucian social system and their activities were eventually curtailed towards the end of the seventeenth century.

In 1771, the Nguyen were overthrown by a revolt led by three brothers from the village of Tay Son, near Hue and in 1786 one of them, Nguyen Hue (no relation to the Nguyen lords), marched north and defeated the Trinh ruler and a supporting Chinese army. Nguyen Hue proclaimed himself Emperor Quang Trung (r. 1788-92) but died on the return march south in 1792. A prince of the Nguyen family, Nguyen Anh, took advantage of the confused situation to seize the southern part of Vietnam aided by the French priest Pigneau de Behaine (1741-99) who attempted to solicit French government help. When they refused to become involved, he turned to French merchants to provide the funds to pay for weapons and mercenaries, Nguyen Anh in return guaranteeing protection for French missionaries. In 1802, the surviving Tay Son rebels were defeated, allowing Nguyen Anh to proclaim himself Emperor Gia Long (r. 1802-20), leader of a united Vietnam and the first ruler of the country's last dynasty. Under Gia Long, Catholicism was tolerated and the emperor even employed Europeans at his court as advisers, although subsequent emperors suppressed Catholicism. The West was again perceived as a threat to the Confucian social order and Catholics − both Vietnamese and European − were persecuted. The government of France, angered by the treatment of its missionaries, demanded protection for them. But the French not only sought protection for their missionaries; they, like the other major European powers, were seeking new markets for their manufactured goods as well as raw materials for industry. Eventually, in 1858, French Emperor Napoleon III (r. 1852-70) ordered Admiral Charles Rigault de Genouilly (1807-73) to mount a naval assault on the port of Tourane (modern-day Da Nang). The attack failed, but de Genouilly sailed south and captured the city of Gia Dinh (in the area of modern-day Ho Chi Minh City). In the next nine years the French gained control of the six provinces of the Mekong Delta, the colony they created becoming known as Cochinchina.

Having landed in northern Vietnam, the French took the city of

Hanoi twice, in 1873 and 1882 and, after the Tonkin Campaign of 1883 to 1886, in which they fought against the Vietnamese, Chinese soldier of fortune Liu Yongfu's (1837-1917) Black Flag Army and the Chinese Guanxi and Yunnan armies, they were in control of the whole of Vietnam. In October 1887, French Indochina was created. It was made up of Annam (Trung Ky, central Vietnam), Tonkin (Bac Ky, northern Vietnam), Cochinchina (Nam Ky, southern Vietnam, and Cambodia, with Laos being added in 1893). Cochinchina enjoyed the status of a colony, Annam was a protectorate with the Nguyen dynasty still in power and Tonkin was controlled by a French governor.

French Colonial Rule

French colonial rule would prove to be harsh and exploitative, the colonial authorities attempting to destroy Vietnamese culture and identity in the name of civilising the people. While the Nguyen monarchy remained in Hue, real power lay in the hands of the French governor general who exercised his authority with ruthless brutality. The French were in Vietnam to exploit the country and Vietnam, therefore, became a supplier of raw materials – rubber, rice and coal – to French industry while indigenous industries were deprived of the opportunity to develop. Villagers, who had worked their small family plots for generations, became little more than low-paid plantation workers or miners, in the employ of French businesses or absentee landlords. Poverty and political repression became rife and the Vietnamese grew increasingly hostile towards the native, Francophile upper class. Unsurprisingly, resistance movements emerged, some led by former court officials, others by peasants. They occasionally revolted, trying to oust the French and re-establish their old, feudal society but by the start of the twentieth century, a new feeling was abroad as young Vietnamese who had never known a pre-colonial Vietnam, became active in the resistance.

Like Chinese reformers of the time, they looked to Japan where a movement known as 'self-strengthening' had become popular in the previous decade. Rather than hold Western technology in disdain, they wanted to harness it to serve Asian needs. The *Dong Du* (Eastern Study) movement was formed by Phan Boi Chau (1867-1940) in 1905, with the objective of sending Vietnamese students to Japan to be educated and prepared to lead an uprising against the French. Arrested by the colonial authorities in 1925, Phan Boi Chau spent the remainder of his life confined to his house in Hue. Political parties were outlawed, but a number of radicals formed clandestine cells. In 1927, the Vietnam Quoc Dan Dong (Vietnamese National Party), modelled after the Chinese Kuomintang, was founded and, three years later, it launched an armed insurrection with attacks on French military posts. Following these attacks, those who did not manage to escape to China were arrested and guillotined.

Ho Chi Minh and the Beginnings of Vietnamese Communism

During this time, three separate Communist parties emerged in Vietnam – the Indochinese Communist Party, the Annamese Communist Party and the Indochinese Communist Union. The Communist International (Comintern) was an organisation, formed in Moscow in 1919, to fight 'for the overthrow of the international bourgeoisie and for the creation of an international Soviet republic'. In 1930, it dispatched a Vietnamese native, Nguyen Ai Quoc ('Nguyen the Patriot') to Hong Kong to coordinate the unification of these parties into one grouping that would become known as the Indochinese Communist Party (ICP). Nguyen Ai Quoc would later be better known to the world as Ho Chi Minh (1890-1969).

He was born as Nguyen Sinh Cung, in northern Annam in 1890. The son of a concubine, his father had studied hard and became a mandarin but would later abandon the imperial court and his family to roam the country as an itinerant teacher and healer. Ho was educated at a French lycée in Hue and was destined to become a teacher. Instead, in 1911, he found work in the galley of a French steamer, the *Amirale de Latouche-Tréville*, under the name Van Ba. It would be thirty years before he would return to his beloved Vietnam. In December 1911, he arrived in the French port of Marseille where he was disappointed by the rejection of his application for the French Colonial Administrative School. Until 1917, therefore, he continued his travelling, often working on ships. In the United States, he lived for a while in New York and Boston, doing menial jobs. During this period, he reportedly lived in London several times, working during one stay at the Carlton Hotel whose chef was the redoubtable Georges Auguste Escoffier (1846-1935), one of the great chefs of the twentieth century. Impressed by the young Vietnamese, Escoffier promoted him to assistant pastry chef. By 1919, Ho was in Paris where many Vietnamese had set up home during the war, working as soldiers or labourers. He worked as a journalist and even had a play he had written performed at the Club de Faubourg. When the Versailles Peace Conference opened, he applied to have US President Woodrow Wilson's (1856-1924) concept of self-determination applied to Vietnam. Although unsuccessful, it was a bold move that attracted the attention of French socialists and, in 1920, Ho was one of the founders of the French Communist Party. In 1924, he travelled to Moscow where he met Stalin (1878-1953), Trotsky (1879-1940) and other prominent communist politicians. Unfortunately, they were too preoccupied with choosing the successor to their late leader, Lenin, to be interested in the fate of Ho's Vietnam.

By 1925, Ho Chi Minh was in southern China, organising youth education classes and lecturing young Vietnamese revolutionaries who were attending the Whampoa Military Academy in Canton. He also worked as an interpreter for the Soviet agent, Mikhail Borodin

(1884-1951), supplementing his income by selling cigarettes and newspapers. Ho was now calling himself Ly Thuy, but was also writing articles for the Soviet news agency and a Chinese newspaper under various pseudonyms. Returning to Moscow in 1927, following Chiang Kai-shek's (1887-1975) anti-communist coup, he toured Europe before heading once again for Asia, arriving in Bangkok in July 1928 and working as a Comintern agent. In 1929, he was in India but a year later returned to Shanghai and, in early 1930 in Hong Kong, he brought together the various organisations that would make the Communist Party of Vietnam. In June 1931, he was arrested by the British but they released him in January 1933. He could next be found working in a restaurant in Milan and then for a few years he was in the Soviet Union recovering from tuberculosis. In 1938, with his influence on the wane amongst members of the Comintern, he was allowed to return to China where he worked as an adviser to the Chinese Communist army.

Thirty years after leaving his native land, he returned, using the name 'Ho Chi Minh' ('He Who Has Been Enlightened'). By this time, he was viewed in Vietnamese revolutionary circles as something of a mythical figure and rumours had even spread that he was dead. As the Germans invaded France and set up the puppet Vichy government there, Ho made contact with leading members of the ICP, men such as Pham Van Dong (1906-2000) – later prime minister of the Democratic Republic of Vietnam (DRV) – and Vo Nguyen Giap (1911-2013) – later defence minister and commander of the Viet Minh and the People's Army of Vietnam. These two men created the League for the Independence of Vietnam (Viet Nam Doc Lap Dong Minh), better known as the Viet Minh. Their objective was to expel from the region both the French and the Japanese who were now being allowed to build military bases in Indochina.

2

The First Indochina War
1946 to 1954

Vietnam at the End of the Second World War

The fall of France at the start of the Second World War left the colonials in Vietnam isolated, forcing them to arrive quickly at an accommodation with the Japanese. In return for being permitted to continue to collect taxes and rents in the colony, they would allow the Japanese to use Indochinese ports, operate airfields in the region and take advantage of the region's raw materials. Other colonial authorities had suffered humiliating defeats in the region, and, with this agreement, the French avoided that, but all depended on the continued success of the Japanese. The war, of course, ended in defeat for Japan but the fact that they initially did so well against the formerly omnipotent colonial powers changed attitudes. The Japanese had presented the conflict as one in which they were fighting on behalf of Asia against Britain and the United States and their initial success empowered local people and movements such as the Viet Minh to believe that they too could be successful in their various struggles for independence.

Based on Tonkin's northern border with China, the Viet Minh spent the war recruiting. They did not use the vocabulary of the social revolutionary, however, insisting instead that they were motivated by the desire for independence and democracy for Vietnam. Their numbers swelled as the region endured famine and people became increasingly unhappy with the actions of their occupiers – both French and Japanese. Vo Nguyen Giap was tasked with turning them into a fighting force. Giap had first met Ho at the lycée in Hue they both attended as teenagers; coincidentally, Ngo Dinh Diem (1901-63), who was President of South Vietnam from 1955 to 1963, attended the same school.

Once France had been liberated in 1944, the Japanese ousted French colonial officials from their positions and, in an effort to curry favour with the people of Vietnam, announced that they were recognising the monarchy, in the form of the Nguyen dynasty's heir, Bao Dai (1913-97). However, when Japan finally surrendered to the Allies on 14 August 1945, there was a power vacuum in Vietnam, giving Ho and his Viet Minh colleagues the opportunity they had been waiting for. In the 'August Revolution', Viet Minh followers seized positions of authority in the cities, towns and villages of the country. Government buildings in Hanoi were occupied and in Hue they marched into the royal palace, demanding the emperor's abdication. On 2 September 1945, Ho Chi Minh mounted a dais in Hanoi's Ba Dinh Square to proclaim the Democratic Republic of Vietnam (DRV). His speech would undoubtedly have pleased the few observers from the American secret service, the Office of Strategic Services (OSS), who were present as he began it by quoting the American Declaration of Independence: 'All men are created equal. They are endowed by their Creator with certain unalienable Rights; among these are Life, Liberty, and the pursuit of Happiness.' Ho was named as Chairman, but his followers were small in number and mostly based in the north of the country and his independent Vietnam was short-lived. The Allies instead decided that the country should be occupied by British and Nationalist Chinese troops who were given the task of disarming the defeated Japanese but were also supportive of Ho's opponents. It appeared that the French were about to return to reinstate the status quo but the situation became confused, with Ho quickly forming a government and appeasing some of his opponents by appointing former Emperor Bao Dai to the position of 'supreme adviser' to the new republic.

The wily Ho promised some seats in the National Assembly for the smaller parties, mainly to encourage the Chinese to believe that all was well and that they could leave. In reality, however, the Viet Minh took most seats. A constitution was drafted but the situation was still unclear. The Viet Minh still had little support in Cochinchina but some supporters made an unsuccessful attempt to seize control of Saigon. British troops occupied parts of the south of the country and limited the activities of the Viet Minh in the city. Meanwhile, militia groups were being formed and there was sporadic fighting between communist and non-communist forces. The Viet Minh remained in control until October 1945 when troops of the *Corps Expéditionnaire Français en Extrême-Orient* (French Far East Expeditionary Force or CEFEO) arrived under the command of General Jacques Leclerc (1902-47) with the task of restoring French rule. With around 50,000 troops, Leclerc began to take control of cities, towns and ports in Vietnam, Cambodia and, eventually, Laos. Realising immediately that total control of Vietnam was impossible, the general recommended to the politicians that the best way to avoid a long conflict would be to negotiate a political solution with the Democratic Republic of Vietnam. Soon, French politician Jean Sainteny (1907-78) seemed to have reached an agreement with Ho Chi Minh, a convention being signed that stated:

'The French government recognises the Republic of Vietnam as a free state which has its government, its parliament, its army, and its finances, and is a part of the Indochinese Federation of the French Union'.

Gareth Power ed., *Vietnam: A History in Documents,*
New York: New American Library, 1981

Concessions had been made. Ho had agreed to allow France to station 25,000 troops in Vietnam until 1951 when they would be withdrawn. He had wanted recognition of his country as an independent state but Sainteny used the term 'free state' instead of 'independent state'. He had, effectively, offered limited independence in the form of local autonomy but only with Vietnam remaining part of the French Union, the new designation for the former French empire. The agreement satisfied no one. Many Vietnamese were dismayed, although they largely remained silent due to the immense esteem in which they held their leader, and French business interests were disappointed by the possibility of losing the colonial privileges they had enjoyed before the war. Ultimately, it did not matter because the agreement was never finalised. On 1 June 1946, France's High Commissioner for Indochina, Admiral Thierry d'Argenlieu (1889-1964), believing that France would prove too strong militarily for the Viet Minh, suddenly announced while the Viet Minh leadership was in Paris engaged in the negotiations, that France was recognising the 'Autonomous Republic of Cochinchina', a puppet French state that was granted the status of a 'free state'. At a meeting in Paris later that summer, it was made clear to the Vietnamese representative, Pham Van Dong, that there would be no more concessions. A frustrated Ho Chi Minh spoke emotionally at a press conference: 'It is Vietnamese soil. It is the flesh of our flesh, the blood of our blood.'

As tension mounted inside Vietnam, there were violent clashes and skirmishes between Viet Minh and French troops in a number of locations, until a confrontation between the Vietnamese and patrol vessels of the French navy at Haiphong resulted in d'Argenlieu ordering an attack on the port at the end of November 1946. The cruiser *Suffren* bombarded Haiphong, resulting in the deaths of a large number of Vietnamese civilians. On 27 November, Ho's government decided to retreat from the cities and, on 19 December, it officially declared war on France. It was the beginning of the First

Indochina War, a conflict that would last for eight years and would end in humiliation for France.

The Viet Minh moved into rural areas and remote mountain locations and reorganised. Vo Nguyen Giap was given command of what was now designated the People's Army of Vietnam (PAVN) and he devised a strategy drawn very much from the war that Chinese Communist leader Mao Zedong (1893-1976) had been fighting. The PAVN, consisting of both a conventional army and the Viet Minh, would not be drawn into set-piece battles where French technological superiority and better equipment could disadvantage them. Instead, they initially fought a guerrilla war, harassing the enemy, damaging his morale and draining him of the will to fight. Meanwhile, Giap sent representatives into villages all over Vietnam to educate the people in the struggle's aims and to ensure that there was popular support for it.

France never committed large numbers of troops to the war, the maximum strength being 192,000 in 1952, and it should also be pointed out that the majority of these troops were drawn from Africa or Indochina. Consequently, there were never more than around 70,000 European soldiers engaged in the fighting. Such a small force meant that, although they were able to remain in control of towns and cities, there was little chance of them being able to devote sufficient resources to controlling more remote rural areas. It rapidly became evident, therefore, that this could become a long and costly conflict and at home, public opinion was far from supportive. The French people were dismayed by the deaths of French soldiers and they were angered by the cost, at a time when France was engaged in re-construction after the devastation caused by the Second World War. At the same time, however, there were some who viewed the situation in Vietnam as an opportunity for France to regain some of the prestige that it had lost in 1940. There were also challenges to French colonial rule in other places such as Madagascar, Morocco and Algeria and it was feared that should

Indochina fall, those colonies would gain confidence that they could also defeat their colonial rulers. Some claimed that Ho was linked inextricably to communism and the perceived ambition of the Soviet Union to achieve world domination and, to more conservative politicians, it was inconceivable that Vietnam should be left to the communists. Such a view was shared by the Truman administration in Washington which resolved to help the French hold onto their colony.

The Fighting Begins

For four years, from 1946 to 1950, the fighting took place mainly in the north, especially in Tonkin, the Vietnamese launching guerrilla-style operations. On 7 October 1947, following the collapse of peace negotiations, the French launched a major offensive, Operation Léa, with the objective of taking the Viet Minh communications centre at Bac Kan and Operation Ceinture was launched thirteen days later. The ambitious objective was the capture of Ho Chi Minh and the defeat of his forces in the north. They failed to find Ho, but succeeded in killing around 7,000 Viet Minh troops and capturing 1,000. This was a major blow to the Communists although the 12,000 French troops were eventually forced to withdraw. Meanwhile, Major General Marcel Alessandri (1895-1968), commander of the French forces, was taking the Red River Delta area that extended north of Hanoi and across to Haiphong on the coast. He failed to consolidate his position fully, however, and the region was fought over for the remainder of the conflict.

In 1949, Mao's communists won victory in China, a critical moment for Hanoi because China would become a vital provider of supplies, weapons and training for the North Vietnamese. On 18 January, China formally recognised the DRV and began to send supplies that amounted by 1953 to around 4,000 tons a month. Now it was time for the Viet Minh to go on the offensive. In February

1950 they launched an operation that captured the French garrison at Lai Khe in Tonkin, close to the Chinese border. Giap next attacked the garrisons at Cao Bang and Dong Khe, capturing them in September and October, respectively, although suffering huge losses in the process. There were losses on the French side, too. 4,800 French troops, evacuated from Cao Bang, died in repeated Viet Minh ambushes. The Viet Minh also captured a huge quantity of equipment including 8,000 rifles. They took many other French outposts and before long were in control of much of northeastern Vietnam.

The French devised a new political strategy, once again involving the former Emperor Bao Dai. On 8 March 1949 in Paris, Bao Dai and the French President Vincent Auriol (1884-1966) signed an agreement that created the State of Vietnam with Saigon as its capital and Bao Dai as head of state. On 1 July 1949, Bao Dai proclaimed Ordinance Number One, effectively the constitution of the new nation. Vietnam now had two governments, one from the Indochina Communist Party and the other with strong allegiances to France and its allies.

On 13 January 1951, the French hit back at the Viet Minh, at Vinh Yen, 30 miles northwest of Hanoi, when around 20,000 PAVN troops attacked 7,000 French. Napalm, supplied to the French by the United States, was deployed for the first time to repel the attackers and on 16 January a major PAVN attack was defeated by French troops and artillery. Other attacks began to threaten Hanoi, but the sheer weight of French firepower inflicted a huge defeat on Giap's men. Around 14,000 PAVN troops were killed, leading to plummeting morale and high levels of desertion. Once again, however, the French failed to consolidate the territory they had gained.

French public opinion was now turning firmly against the war, making it essential for them to achieve a victory as swiftly as possible. They launched an offensive aimed at taking Hoa Binh, a city to the south of the Red River delta. Three parachute battalions secured the city, with the Viet Minh retreating as usual. They assembled five divisions and deployed two of them against French supply routes to Hoa Binh. The fighting was brutal around the city, the French losing 894 troops and the Viet Minh considerably more, estimated at around 6,000. Relentless Viet Minh attacks eventually persuaded the French to withdraw and then, on 23 March, Giap attacked Mao Khe, 20 miles north of Haiphong. Five days of brutal hand-to-hand fighting ensued before the Vietnamese commander withdrew his men, having lost 3,000 of them, according to the French. The following day he unleashed his troops on Phu Ly, Ninh Binh and Phat Diem, south of Hanoi. Each of these attacks was repulsed by the French whose new commander, General Jean de Lattre de Tassigny (1889-1952) launched a counter-offensive, driving the demoralised Viet Minh back into the jungle and killing around 10,000. The previous year, de Lattre had established a fortified line stretching from Hanoi to the Gulf of Tonkin – the 'De Lattre Line' – that was intended to keep the enemy in place while allowing the French to attack them. Giap was unable to breach this line and, as the number of casualties rose, doubts were raised about his conduct of the war. In January 1952, however, de Lattre was struck down by cancer and returned to France where he died. His replacement was General Raoul Salan (1899-1984) who almost immediately faced attacks at Hoa Binh that pushed the French back to the De Lattre Line. Thousands more died on each side. There were no further major offensives in 1952 and the French, desperate to engage the enemy in a conventional battle instead of relentless ambushes, initiated what were called 'hedgehog' tactics. By this strategy, well-defended outposts were set up in the hope that they would draw the Viet Minh from the jungle. But Giap was now enjoying some success, controlling most of Tonkin beyond the De Lattre Line.

The DRV general changed tack in 1953, invading Laos and overrunning several French outposts, leading to Salan's replacement by General Henri Navarre as supreme commander of French forces in Indochina. Navarre immediately reported back to his government that there was no possibility of winning the war, and that stalemate was about the best that could be hoped for. Deciding to employ his predecessor's 'hedgehog' tactics to block the Viet Minh's invasion of Laos, Navarre selected the small town of Dien Bien Phu, 10 miles north of the Laos border. On 20 November 1953, French troops parachuted in, easily wiping out the Viet Minh garrison and seizing control of the valley which was 12 miles long, 8 miles wide and surrounded by wooded hills. But Navarre had underestimated the ability and strategic planning of the Viet Minh who realised that a resounding victory would weaken the French and give Ho and his colleagues a good position from which to argue at the forthcoming Geneva Conference on Vietnam's future. So, rather than using their customary guerrilla tactics, Giap devised a more conventional attack, using artillery and infantry designed to isolate the garrison. America had considered a conventional attack to relieve the French at Dien Bien Phu – bombs dropped from planes taking off from aircraft carriers in the Gulf of Tonkin, Okinawa and the Philippines. But, significantly, Operation Vulture, as this proposed initiative was known, was rejected by President Dwight D. Eisenhower (1890-1969) after the British refused to participate. He was also reluctant to escalate American involvement in the conflict by using American pilots. On 7 May, the French at Dien Bien Phu surrendered with the loss of around 2,000 dead, 6,650 wounded and 1,729 missing. Of 10,863 taken prisoner, only 3,290 survived.

The DRV's success at Dien Bien Phu was a catastrophe for France but was also a major setback for American objectives in the region. Not only would it allow China and the Soviet Union to advance their ambitions, the United States' credibility suffered a severe blow. This would have serious implications for both America's allies and her enemies.

The United States and the First French-Indochina War

Immediately after the Second World War, Europe entered a period of instability as the Soviet Union began its domination of Eastern Europe and the Cold War began. As the Russians sought to safeguard their own frontiers and exploit the economic resources of the countries of the east, America championed the notion of a free and open Europe. Their ideological conflict – communism against capitalism – was reflected in situations around the world and nowhere more dramatically than in Korea. The invasion of South Korea by forces of the North on 25 June 1950 encouraged the United States to support France's struggle in Indochina. Meanwhile, the Americans were helping Greece and Turkey to defeat communist uprisings and President Truman, who had succeeded Franklin Roosevelt in the White House, pledged to support any nation threatened by what he termed 'totalitarianism'. The Americans had invented the 'domino theory', the notion that if Indochina were allowed to become communist, the other countries of Southeast Asia would soon follow suit. While having no intention of supporting French colonial ambitions, the Americans wanted to keep communism at bay. At the time, it must be remembered that the United States was in the grip of a 'Red Scare' that manifested itself in a number of ways. The fact that the Soviet Union now had the bomb, having tested an atomic device in late 1949, created a kind of hysteria. Spy trials – those of the Rosenbergs, Julius (1918-53) and Ethel (1915-53), and Alger Hiss – hogged the newspaper headlines and, in February 1950, Senator Joseph McCarthy roused anti-communist and anti-Soviet Union sentiments when he began to allege that communists had infiltrated many areas of American society.

When both China and the Soviet Union recognised the Democratic Republic of Vietnam, headed by Ho Chi Minh, the

United States' attitude to France's war in Indochina changed immediately. The policy of providing support to France – begun by President Harry S. Truman (1884-1972) and continued by his successor, Dwight D. Eisenhower – was not without its opponents, however. France's colonial ambitions remained anathema to most American policy-makers but how else could the Chinese and the Soviets be prevented from advancing their interests in the region? By the beginning of 1954, the United States was funding around 80 per cent of France's military expenditure in Indochina.

Thus, Indochina became the focus of the struggle to restrict communism in the Far East and, when China began to arm the North Vietnamese and provide economic aid, it seemed from an American point of view that the decision to support the French had indeed been a good one. Now the conflict could be dressed up as a war of containment and not colonisation. On 7 February 1950, the United States recognised the State of Vietnam and $10 million of military aid was pledged to France. In September, President Truman dispatched a Military Assistance Advisory Group (MAAG) to Vietnam to advise the French.

But, as we have seen, things did not go well for the French from the outset. Following the setbacks they suffered between 1950 and 1952, American aid was substantially increased, especially in view of the fact that the Americans were trying to obtain French support for their plans for the defence of Western Europe, plans that included the re-arming of Germany, an idea that was anathema to many French citizens who had suffered at the hands of the Germans in two world wars. The United States wanted France to continue to take the lead in Vietnam as American efforts were already focused on Korea and Europe. That would soon change.

3

Keeping the Dominoes Standing: President Eisenhower 1954 to 1960

The Geneva Conference

In 1954, a year after the installation of Eisenhower as President of the United States, France's eight-year struggle in Vietnam came to an end. The United States remained reluctant to let the communists win, however, and sought to maintain a foothold in that part of the world, especially as Indochina was also an important trading region. Having provided substantial aid to the French – some $3 billion over the course of the conflict – Eisenhower's government now elected to do the same for opponents of Ho Chi Minh's Democratic Republic of Vietnam. The leader behind whom it decided to put its considerable resources was Ngo Dinh Diem.

Eisenhower had an illustrious war record as Supreme Allied Commander in Europe and, under President Truman, had commanded NATO forces. He believed firmly that the world was in the grip of a struggle between freedom and communist-inspired tyranny, and Vietnam and Southeast Asia were, therefore, to his mind non-negotiable. Times were tough, however. He had won the presidency with a promise of reduced government expenditure, including military spending. Therefore, instead of throwing money and resources at difficult situations, his administration sought to form regional military alliances backed up with the threat of nuclear warfare to provide a compelling argument to any country that did not fall into line.

The Americans were dismayed when France accepted a proposal from the Soviet Union for a conference in Geneva in April 1954 to discuss both Korea and Vietnam. Present would be France, the United States, the Soviet Union, Britain and China. The Americans attended reluctantly, fearful that if they did not, the French would withdraw from Southeast Asia anyway. They were also still trying to persuade the French government to accept the notion of the European Defence Community and the re-arming of Germany. Eisenhower was in a quandary, fearful, as he conceded to a reporter at a press conference on 7 April 1954, that the 'domino principle' would now come into effect. He said, 'you have a row of dominoes set up. You knock over the first one, and what will happen to the last one is the certainty that it will go over very quickly.' With little political will in the United States for a unilateral intervention, however, the president explored instead the possibility of multinational action, claiming that, 'It would be a great mistake for the President of the United States to enter the fray in partnership only with France.' He wrote to the British Prime Minister, Sir Winston Churchill (1874-1965), but there was no will to do anything before the Geneva Conference.

At Geneva, Eisenhower elected to merely observe rather than participate. The Viet Minh victory at Dien Bien Phu had guaranteed that the French would readily accept a compromise agreement and the US president was unwilling to be part of anything that seemed to be a compromise with communists. The result was that France and the Democratic Republic of Vietnam concluded a ceasefire and Vietnam was, effectively, partitioned – the DRV would control the country north of the 17th Parallel while France would retain control of the area south of that line. A demilitarised zone (DMZ) about 6 miles wide would act as a buffer between the two. This would only be a temporary arrangement, however. The Geneva Agreements called for an election throughout Vietnam in July 1956 to determine who would govern the country. At that point, France would leave.

The First Indochina War was at an end and, after 92 years, France withdrew from the region. In the seven years and seven months of the war, more than 75,000 French troops had lost their lives and their allies – the State of Vietnam, Laos and Cambodia – had lost more than 18,000. Between 175,000 and 300,000 Viet Minh had died.

They would be far from the last to die in Vietnam's struggle for unification and self-determination.

Ngo Dinh Diem

United States Secretary of State, John Foster Dulles (1888-1959), had called for 'united action' in March 1954 when the French were besieged at Dien Bien Phu and, immediately after the Geneva Conference ended, the United States again began working towards a multilateral approach. The result was a regional defence alliance between America, Britain, Australia, New Zealand, the Philippines, France, Thailand and Pakistan. Known as the Southeast Asia Treaty Organisation (SEATO) or occasionally the Manila Pact, it was created primarily to block communist advancement in Southeast Asia. It bore some comparison, obviously, with the North Atlantic Treaty Organisation (NATO) but did not commit members as fully to action as that agreement did. It did, however, provide a vehicle for discussion of joint action in situations such as had occurred at Dien Bien Phu. The Geneva Agreements prevented Vietnam, Laos or Cambodia from participating in military alliances although they were considered to be under the protection of SEATO and the organisation proved useful to Presidents Eisenhower, Kennedy, Johnson and Nixon who used it to justify United States military involvement in the region.

Unwilling to recognise the DRV, the United States was left with limited options; either it used force against the Viet Minh or it came to a negotiated settlement with Ho Chi Minh's government. Meanwhile, Washington was firmly of the opinion that the Viet Minh success in the recent conflict was more to do with the weakness of the French – both politically and militarily – than the strength of the forces of the Democratic Republic of Vietnam.

To establish some stability in the State of Vietnam, President Eisenhower sent General J. Lawton 'Lightning Joe' Collins (1896-1987), one of his most important field commanders during the Second World War, to Saigon. Usefully, Collins spoke French and was personally acquainted with General Paul-Henri-Romuald Ely (1897-1975), the French High Commissioner in Indochina. His first task was to identify a leader who could stand up to the Viet Minh but would also be capable of creating a regime amenable to western interests. Bao Dai's prime minister was Ngo Dinh Diem but he was unpopular and untried. He was distrusted because he had been appointed prime minister by an emperor who was viewed by many Vietnamese as merely a puppet of the French. Furthermore, Ho and the DRV were admired by many in the State of Vietnam, because they had won such an outstanding victory at Dien Bien Phu and had been accorded recognition at Geneva. In order to make the staunchly anti-communist Diem more acceptable, Collins decided that he would have to be given more independence of action by the French.

But Diem had long been a thorn in the flesh of the French. In 1933, he had resigned from his position as Bao Dai's Interior Minister, just three months into the job, after unsuccessfully demanding that the French introduce a Vietnamese legislature. In 1949, he refused a seat in Bao Dai's cabinet, again because he disliked French rule. To Ho and the Viet Minh, he and his powerful family were hated rivals and it is likely that they were responsible for the death of Diem's older brother, Ngo Dinh Khoi (1885-1945), in 1945. Diem was himself under constant threat of assassination by them. His views were in line with those of the United States; he was vehemently anti-communist as well as opposed to colonialism but he was never loved by the Vietnamese people. A cold distant man, he displayed none of the personal qualities required of a politician. He was very devout, from a family of Roman Catholics and was supported by the small number of Roman Catholics in Vietnam where the majority of people were, of course, Buddhists. Despite being suspicious of him, Bao Dai appointed Diem prime minister in June 1954. It has been suggested by some sources that the Americans were behind this appointment, but there is no evidence to prove this. It seems more likely that Bao Dai made the appointment to garner American support in the face of France's imminent exit from the region. It was part of Collins' mission in Saigon to examine Diem's suitability for the office and whether he could offer the people of Vietnam a viable alternative to the communists. Unfortunately, he reported back to Washington that Diem was incapable of providing the strong leadership that Vietnam needed. This was something of a surprise to John Foster Dulles who had already received a contrary opinion from Colonel Edward G. Lansdale (1908-87) who had been working alongside Diem in Saigon. Nonetheless, Collins' opinion prevailed and it was decided to focus less on Diem and start to work with other Vietnamese anti-communist political figures. Before this could be acted upon, however, fighting erupted in Saigon. On 28 April, armed members of religious sects and gangsters moved against the Vietnamese National Army. The uprising was quashed but, in such an atmosphere of crisis, it was decided that this was not the right moment to begin to introduce political change. US policy changed to one of unflinching support for Diem and depended, until 1963, on him being able to provide effective government for Vietnam.

Meanwhile, Ho Chi Minh was preoccupied with his own internal turmoil. Hanoi had launched a programme of agrarian reform in 1953, aimed at reducing rents and re-distributing land from large landowners and rich peasants to those poorer than them. It has been estimated that between 120,000 and 200,000 landowners were executed, although it is claimed that many were killed in error and were little more than poor peasants. In the leader's home province, Nghe An, a peasant revolt against the land reforms resulted in 6,000 deaths. There would later be a public apology by the government for the campaign's excesses.

Diem ousts Bao Dai

Despite SEATO, America now stood alone in the task of creating a viable nation in South Vietnam. There were a number of obstacles to this, Diem's lack of ability notwithstanding. There was a monarch in place who possessed little credibility, living, as he did, the life of a playboy in the South of France. The Vietnamese National Army – around 150,000 strong – was badly led and inexperienced, too. There was inexperience at the heart of government; French colonial rule had left to their own devices people with no experience of decision-making or managing government departments. The country had little industry and those who worked the land had for decades been victims of absentee landlords, punitive taxes and crippling debt. Unsurprisingly, they had little time for a government in Saigon that had collaborated with the French. Nonetheless, an important part of the Geneva Accords was an election set for July 1956. The only problem was that, if a free vote was allowed to take place, Ho Chi Minh would undoubtedly be the victor and that was the last thing that Washington wanted to see happen.

Part of Diem's problem, as we have noted, was that he had been appointed by Bao Dai and was tainted by the emperor's connection with French colonial rule. Therefore, it came as something of a surprise when Diem suddenly announced a referendum in October 1955 to decide whether or not to depose Bao Dai. He won a substantial vote in favour of the deposition of the monarch – not without substantial ballot rigging by his brothers Ngo Dinh Nhu (1910-63) and Ngo Dinh Can (1911-64) – and became president of what was now the Republic of Vietnam.

South Vietnam began to move inexorably towards dictatorship, as Diem's brothers worked assiduously behind the scenes, using vote-rigging, bribery and threats to gain support for him. Village councils, made up of elected officials, were replaced by representatives of Diem's government and those opposed to the new president were sent to camps to be 're-educated'. Lansdale, a close friend of Diem, supported this action, justifying it as necessary in the establishment of centralised control in the country. Meanwhile, Collins continued to oppose this view, believing the Ngo clan was merely working for its own benefit. Nonetheless, US support for Diem continued unabated, quarter of a billion dollars flooding into Vietnam's coffers every year in the late 1950s, most of it destined for the Army of the Republic of Vietnam (ARVN) and not for what was really needed – agricultural and industrial development. But the American personnel commitment was still minimal and before 1961 there were only around 900 uniformed American troops in Vietnam, acting as advisers to the Army of the Republic of Vietnam.

Diem visited the United States in May 1957 and was feted wherever he went, in a trip that was little more than a PR stunt designed to create the impression that America's involvement in Vietnam was providing positive results. His request to Eisenhower for an increase in aid was, however, declined. There were still arguments about the way in which aid was being allocated. The US ambassador to Vietnam, Elbridge Durbrow, was of the opinion that the best way for Diem's regime to gain credibility and support was to spend more on schemes that would foster economic development and political reform. He encouraged Washington to withhold funds until such improvements were implemented but US officials such as Lansdale, now a brigadier-general, resisted such arguments, claiming that, until the enemy was eradicated, such reforms should take a back seat. They prevailed and US support for Diem continued.

While acts of terrorism and anti-government violence were on the increase in the south during the late 1950s, Ho Chi Minh was ordering his operatives there to avoid violence and use propaganda and persuasion instead. He feared American military retaliation if it was thought that the violence was emanating from Hanoi. Nonetheless, the Viet Minh in the south often ignored such orders and engaged in acts of violence against government representatives and the army. But, with frustration increasing, a resolution was finally passed in Hanoi in January 1959 by the Central Committee of the Vietnam Workers Party accepting the notion of 'protracted armed struggle' to overthrow the Diem government in the south. Four months later, work began on the construction of what would come to be known as the 'Ho Chi Minh Trail', a system of secret routes into South Vietnam by which troops, weaponry and supplies could be transported. It ran from the north into Laos and then into South Vietnam's Central Highlands and is regarded as one of the great military engineering achievements of the twentieth century. On 20 December 1960, party operatives created the National Liberation Front for South Vietnam (NLF), a force not unlike the Viet Minh that would be made up of southern insurgents controlled by the Hanoi government. It created yet another problem for the Diem regime which, in early 1961, was described by Brigadier-General Lansdale as being in 'critical condition'. He warned that the NLF had 'started to steal the country and expect it to be done in 1961'.

4

Unwavering Commitment:
President Kennedy
1961 to 1963

A Worrying Legacy

Eisenhower had succeeded in preventing Vietnam from being taken
over by the communists – had, in effect, kept the domino standing.
The legacy that he left to the next President of the United States,
the young senator from Massachusetts, John F. Kennedy (1917-
63), however, was a far from satisfactory one. The nation that his
government had tried to build in the south of Vietnam still depended
on American support; its government was weak and it faced the very
real prospect of collapse in the face of the threat from the National
Liberation Front for South Vietnam. Kennedy was of the same mind
as the previous incumbent of his new office, describing Vietnam in
a speech as the 'finger in the dike' that was holding back 'the red
tide of communism' in the region. In 1956, he had described South
Vietnam as 'the cornerstone of the free world in Southeast Asia'.
But it was obvious that the policy of containment designed to be
brought about by the development of the Republic of Vietnam was
not working.

To make matters worse, the new president's first months in office
were difficult as he dealt with crises in Berlin, where the Russians
built the Berlin Wall, and in Cuba where a revolution had taken
place on America's doorstep and a botched invasion at the Bay of Pigs
had severely damaged the nation's perception of Kennedy. Sensing
that the public was beginning to think that they had elected the

wrong man, he decided to use Vietnam as the focus for anti-Soviet and anti-Chinese activity. He authorised an increase in the ARVN's strength to 200,000 and 400 US Army Special Forces troops – the famous Green Berets – were dispatched to South Vietnam's Central Highlands to train local Montagnard tribesmen. US Vice President Lyndon Johnson (1908-73) travelled to Saigon to meet with Diem and for the first time Kennedy began to consider sending combat troops to Vietnam, commissioning a report on the matter by the Pentagon.

The NLF, meanwhile, persevered with its propaganda in the villages of the south, Ho and his advisers having been made aware that their backers in Moscow were reluctant to see the conflict escalate militarily. Activity on the Ho Chi Minh Trail increased and soon there were 10,000 men and women in the National Liberation Front, soon to become better known as the 'Viet Cong'. As attacks increased, even in the area around the capital, General Maxwell Taylor (1901-1987) and Deputy National Security Adviser Walt Rostow (1916-2003), sent by Kennedy to Saigon to report on the situation, recommended not just an increase in military, economic and advisory support but also that a US military task force of 8,000 troops be sent to Vietnam. Kennedy rejected the notion of sending combat troops but did accept that increased aid was needed. Consequently, in December 1961, 33 Shawnee helicopters, their pilots and 400 maintenance technicians were transported to South Vietnam, and US aircraft carriers began to patrol off the Vietnamese coast, occasionally inside Vietnamese territorial waters. This meant that US military personnel were going into action, attacking Viet Cong positions, while US Special Forces troops were accompanying and advising ARVN troops in covert operations. As a result, the first American casualties were incurred, and 216 US military personnel had lost their lives by the end of 1964, more than double the number of the previous year.

Meanwhile, State Department officials such as George Ball (1909–

1994), Averell Harriman (1891-1986) and Chester Bowles (1901-86) argued that it would be better to negotiate with the government of the DRV. But US Secretary of Defense Robert McNamara (1916-2009) remained optimistic that the plan was working and, indeed, ARVN troops had come out on top against Viet Cong positions in the Mekong Delta and around the capital. Faced with a choice between negotiating and carrying on as before, however, Kennedy instead opted for what he called 'limited partnership'.

Assassination

In December 1961, there were 3,000 American military advisers in Vietnam but, by 1962, that number had reached 9,000 and military aid had also been substantially increased. A new authority, Military Assistance Command Vietnam (MACV) was set up to manage the increasingly complex aid effort. In a bid to combat the insurgency in the countryside, MACV worked with the ARVN to establish around 3,000 'strategic hamlets' in which villagers would be free of Viet Cong influence and violence. These would be militarily secure, but to create them, many people had to be relocated and forced labour was used to build them, leading to a great deal of discontent. In fact, they were never really fit for purpose, only around 10 per cent of them having any proper security. There were also very few young men in the families herded into the strategic hamlets; they had all enlisted with the NLF. The promises of supplies and services remained unfulfilled while occupants lived in poor conditions and were subject to harassment, arrest and extortion. NLF members infiltrated them at night and continued to exert a powerful influence, describing such villages as little more than prisons and using them as a recruiting tool. For a while, Washington believed that progress was at last being made in Vietnam but that perception was soon shattered. On 2 January 1963, at Ap Bac, to the southwest of Saigon, an ARVN force, ten times the size of its opponents, equipped with sophisticated American weaponry and supported by air cover, was decisively defeated by an NLF battalion. The ARVN soldiers were badly led and reluctant to fight, an indication of the low esteem in which the government of the Republic of Vietnam was held. Many of the officers were excessively cautious, as Diem was in the habit of doling out harsh criticism to those who incurred even small numbers of casualties. To make matters worse, in the chaos of orders that were misunderstood or simply ignored, 5 US helicopters were downed and 65 ARVN and 3 US personnel were killed. For the NLF it was a major victory that provided them with a massive boost.

Around this time, the real contempt for the Diem government was displayed in images of burning Buddhist monks who set themselves on fire in protest at the oppression the Vietnamese people were enduring and the favouritism shown to Roman Catholics by the government. The horrific pictures – especially that of Thich Quang Duc (1897-1963), photographed at the moment of his self-immolation by Malcolm Browne (1931-2012) who won a Pulitzer Prize for his picture – appeared in the media around the globe. It seemed obvious now to the Americans that they would have to consider the removal of the Diem regime. On 24 August 1963, therefore, a cable was sent to the US ambassador to Vietnam, Henry Cabot Lodge Jr (1902-1985), instructing him to order Diem to sack his hated brother, Ngo Dinh Nhu, from his government position. Nhu headed Diem's secret police and police attacks on Buddhist temples were being carried out under his orders. The cable went on to instruct the ambassador to let it be known in the right circles that America would not stand in the way of a coup attempt. Diem refused to get rid of his brother, leaving Kennedy with no choice but to implement the recommendations in a report drafted by General Maxwell Taylor and Defense Secretary, Robert McNamara, who had held discussions with Diem in Saigon in October. The report recommended withholding various types of US aid to South Vietnam, including a reduction of 1,000 in the number of US advisers. This threat frightened the Vietnamese generals into staging a coup and the United States, having all but abandoned Diem by this time, merely stood back and watched. The generals seized power on 1 November 1963 and Diem and Nhu were both murdered.

Just twenty-two days later, the world reeled in shock when President Kennedy was assassinated by Lee Harvey Oswald in Dallas and, consequently, we will never know how he would have dealt with Vietnam in the remaining year of his tenure of the Oval Office or, indeed, what would have happened had he secured re-election in 1964. Some have claimed that he had devised a plan for American withdrawal from Vietnam and they use the proposed reduction in advisers as evidence of that. His focus on the defeat of communism in Indochina, however, would seem to contradict this and he did make more of a commitment in terms of personnel and military aid than Eisenhower ever did. After all, when he took office, there were 800 US military personnel in Vietnam but, by the time he died, there were 16,700. One need only look at his inaugural address in 1961 to understand the depth of his commitment to keeping South Vietnam free of communists and to believe that his presidency should hold some responsibility for the way the situation subsequently evolved:

'The United States will pay any price, bear any burden, meet any hardship, support any friend, oppose any foe to assure the survival and the success of liberty.'

5

Other Belligerents
1962 to 1975

Australia

Australia had also been involved in advising the ARVN, having dispatched 30 military advisers in 1962. Its growing involvement resulted from a fear of the spread of communism in the region and Diem had been feted when he visited the country in 1957. As well as being a member of SEATO, of course, Australia had signed up to the Australia, New Zealand, United States Treaty (ANZUS), a military alliance that committed Australia to cooperate with the United States on defence in the Pacific Ocean area.

The Australian army had gained invaluable experience of jungle fighting and counter-insurgency while assisting the British army in Malaya during the Malayan Emergency, a guerrilla war fought between forces of the Commonwealth and the communist Malayan National Liberation Army between 1948 and 1960. The Australian Army Training Team Vietnam (AATTV or 'the Team') arrived in Vietnam between July and August 1962 and, two years later, Australia augmented its personnel and equipment in Vietnam with the arrival of a flight of Caribou transports. By the end of 1964, there were around 200 Australian military personnel in the country. Towards the end of that year, Australian Prime Minister Robert Menzies (1894-1978) announced the introduction of conscription for 20-year-olds and, indeed, many conscripted men would serve in Vietnam. In April 1965, Menzies announced that, in response to a request for more military help from the government of the Republic of Vietnam, Australia would be sending troops. His view was that the insurgency was a threat to the security of Australia. 'It must be seen,' he said, 'as part of a thrust by Communist China between the Indian and Pacific Oceans.'

Australian operational methods differed greatly to those of the Americans and to prevent confusion it was decided to limit Australian troops to an area where they could, in effect, fight their own war, using their own tactics. In April 1966, therefore, the two infantry battalions – later increased to three – of 1st Australian Task Force moved into Phuoc Tuy Province, north of Saigon. The Royal Australian Air Force also increased in strength to three squadrons – one of Caribou, one of Iroquois helicopters and one of Canberra bombers. The bombers carried out numerous raids while the Caribou and Iroquois were used in supporting and transporting ground forces. A destroyer of the Royal Australian Navy (RAN) was used in a coastal bombardment role.

One of the best-known engagements involving Australian forces was the Battle of Long Tan on 18 and 19 August 1966. During this incident, a heavily outnumbered company of Australian troops inflicted a decisive defeat on a regiment-sized force of Viet Cong with the loss of 18 men. At least 245 Viet Cong died in the battle. After this battle, there were further large engagements but the Viet Cong rarely posed any great challenges for the Australians in Phuoc Tuy Province again. In one week in February 1967, however, during Operation Bribie, designed to clear Viet Cong from rainforest north of Ap My An, 16 Australians lost their lives and 55 were wounded. As a result of these losses, a third battalion arrived in December of that year. By early 1968, there were 8,000 Australian troops in Vietnam, the highest number of the entire conflict. During the Tet Offensive, in early 1968, 22 Australian soldiers were killed, leading to the kind of protests in Australia that had been happening in the United States. Meanwhile, the growing doubts about

American commitment to Southeast Asia created uncertainty in the Australian government and Prime Minister John Gorton (1911-2002) announced that there would be no increase in the number of Australian troops in Vietnam. Nonetheless, the fighting continued and, in May, 25 Australian soldiers died during the Battle of Coral-Balmoral. One of the last large-scale actions Australian forces were involved in was the Battle of Binh Ba fought between 6 and 8 June 1969 in which the communists suffered such heavy losses that they decided to move out of Phuoc Tuy Province into neighbouring areas. The Australians did not become involved in such major engagements again.

Withdrawal of Australian troops began in November 1970 and the last Australian infantry battalion sailed home on 9 December 1971. Advisers remained until 11 January 1973 when Australia announced the end of combat operations against the communists. 521 Australian troops had died and approximately 3,000 were wounded.

South Korea
The second-largest contingent of troops after the Americans fighting the communists was that of South Korea. President Kennedy had rejected an offer of help from them in 1961, but Lyndon Johnson requested their participation in 1964. From then until 1973 they sent more than 300,000 troops to Vietnam. They were considered to be a highly effective force especially in their conduct of counter-insurgency operations. Just over 5,000 South Korean troops lost their lives in Vietnam and almost 11,000 were injured.

New Zealand
This was the first conflict in which New Zealand forces did not fight alongside British and their involvement in the war caused widespread protest. Troops were sent in 1965 as a result of treaty commitments under the terms of the ANZUS pact with Australia

and the United States, but the government also had concerns about the spread of communism in the region. The government elected to become only minimally involved, especially as their commitments in Malaya were stretching their military resources.

Philippines, Thailand and Taiwan

Philippines sent 10,450 troops to Vietnam who mostly participated in medical and civilian pacification. Its major naval base, Subic Bay, was the home of the US Seventh Fleet from 1964 until the end of the Vietnam War in 1975. Taiwan provided military training personnel and ran a covert cargo transport operation while Thai troops fought in Vietnam between 1965 and 1971, especially in the covert operations in Laos.

6

Americanising the War: President Johnson 1963 to 1968

A New President

Of the presidents who had to deal with the situation in Vietnam, from Truman to Ford, Lyndon Johnson was the one to whom the responsibility for escalating it into an all-out fighting war against the Democratic Republic of Vietnam must be ascribed. Johnson had, of course, come to power in unfortunate circumstances following the assassination of President Kennedy, but the Senator from Texas had always been an ambitious man. He believed in the ideals of reform and equality that had been launched in the 1930s with Roosevelt's 'New Deal' and now conceived of what he termed the 'Great Society', an America in which every citizen shared in and benefited from the nation's great wealth. He also wholeheartedly supported America's role as leader in what he saw as the global fight against communism and tyranny. Consequently, he believed implicitly in the American mission in Vietnam and the ability of American power to defeat what he described on one occasion as a 'raggedy-ass little fourth-rate country'. He was adamant that Vietnam would not fall to the communists, telling White House aides that he did not want Moscow and Beijing to think that 'we're yellow and we don't mean what we say'. The problem was, of course, that he faced an implacable enemy prepared to make any sacrifice in the struggle for self-determination and equally convinced of the justice of its cause. As Johnson's presidency went on, however, and the body count, as well as the cost of the war increased, the American people would begin to doubt whether it was all worth it and to question whether Lyndon Baines Johnson was, indeed, the right man for the job.

Naturally, following Kennedy's death, there was a chance that the communist world would believe America to be weakened. Just a few days after the assassinated president's funeral, therefore, Johnson sought to deal quickly with such thinking by signing National Security Action Memorandum No. 273, a reiteration of the United States' pledge to help the South Vietnamese 'to win their contest against the externally directed and supported communist conspiracy'. Following the coup and the murder of Diem, the Republic of Vietnam was now led by a military committee headed by Duong Van 'Big' Minh and Johnson instructed his ambassador in Saigon, Henry Cabot Lodge, to let the new RVN leaders know that during his presidency the United States would stick to its promise. At the same time, however, Johnson had no intention of letting the conflict evolve into a major war and he always sought to ensure that there was just enough firepower available even as his generals repeatedly requested increases as things got worse.

The strategic hamlets policy had failed miserably, since people were understandably reluctant to be moved from the homes and land where their families had lived and worked for centuries. Corrupt management of the system by government officials did not help. Meanwhile, the men and equipment smuggled along the Ho Chi Minh Trail had greatly increased and, in fact, by the end of Johnson's first year in office, the NLF were in control of large areas of South Vietnam. In an effort to effect a change in the way the war was being conducted, Johnson appointed one of the best American military minds to the command of MACV – General William C. Westmoreland (1914-2005). Westmoreland – described by Johnson as 'the best we have, without question' – immediately requested more troops and the number of US advisers working with the ARVN rose to more than 23,000. With the advice of his aides, many of whom had served under President Kennedy, Johnson also changed his focus away from the NLF and towards Hanoi. In the opinion of men such as Robert McNamara, Dean Rusk and Walt Rostow, Hanoi was the place from which the communist war effort was emanating. Covert operations, under the codename Operation 34A or OPLAN 34Alpha, and directed by the US Central Intelligence Agency, were launched in the north and a series of secret commando raids by South Vietnamese troops on the coast of North Vietnam were designed to gather information and spread anti-communist propaganda. Hanoi complained to the International Control Commission that had been created in 1954 to ensure that the terms of the Geneva Accords were being adhered to, but when challenged, the Americans simply denied involvement in the coastal attacks. They made little difference, however, apart from an increase in NLF activity. It was becoming increasingly apparent that the only way to put the required pressure on Hanoi would be to employ American air power. Of course, with the world looking on and American credibility at stake, this could not be done without some provocation. Before long, however, Johnson had his provocation.

The Gulf of Tonkin Incident

On the afternoon of 2 August 1964, the USS *Maddox*, a twenty-year-old destroyer, was patrolling the waters of the Gulf of Tonkin, off the coast of North Vietnam. The vessel was on what were called DESOTO (**DE** Haven **S**pecial **O**perations off **T**singta**O**) operations, first performed off the coast of China by USS *De Haven*, conducted in hostile waters to gather intelligence. In command of US forces in the area, on board his flagship USS *Bon Homme Richard*, was Captain George Morrison (1919-2008), father of the soon-to-be-famous Doors front man, Jim Morrison. Patrolling inside a 14-mile limit claimed by North Vietnam – a limit not recognised by the

US government – the *Maddox* came under attack from three North Vietnamese Navy P-4 torpedo boats. The message received at the Pentagon stated that, after the *Maddox* had taken evasive action when torpedoes were fired at her, she retaliated by opening fire with her 127 millimetre guns. Two of the torpedo boats had come within 6 miles of the American vessel and each had unleashed a torpedo. The other North Vietnamese boat received a direct hit from the *Maddox*. In addition, four American F-8 Crusader jets that had been ordered to take off from the aircraft carrier, the USS *Ticonderoga,* strafed the retreating P-4s. It was claimed that one had been sunk and the other had been seriously damaged, while the North Vietnamese claimed that they had downed one aircraft and that the *Maddox* had, in fact, been hit by one of the torpedoes. An NSA historical study in 2005 has a slightly altered version of the events which has the *Maddox* opening fire first, firing three warning rounds at the torpedo boats. At the time, however, the US government maintained that the North Vietnamese had been the aggressors and these warning shots were not reported. Then, on 4 August, while on another patrol off the North Vietnamese coast, the *Maddox* and the USS *Turner Joy* received radar, sonar and radio signals that they believed were an indication of another attack by vessels of the North Vietnamese navy. The two ships used these signals to plot the locations of the enemy ships and opened fire. Although they claimed that they sank two torpedo boats, no physical evidence of this was ever found.

Despite the vagueness of reports about a second attack, and in spite of stating privately in 1965 that, 'For all I know, our Navy was shooting at whales out there', Johnson now had all the provocation he needed. Within half an hour of the second 'attack' he had decided on American retaliation, ordering air strikes. Meanwhile, via the 'hot line' between Washington and Moscow, he reassured Leonid Brezhnev (1906-82) that he had no intention of widening the war in Vietnam. Late on 4 August, in a radio broadcast to the American people, Johnson described the two incidents and demanded the authority to undertake retaliatory measures. No mention was made of the US vessels' proximity to the North Vietnamese coast. The president chose, rather, to describe them as having been on the 'high seas', implying that they were in international waters when attacked.

On 7 August, the United States Congress passed the Southeast Asia Resolution (the Tonkin Gulf Resolution), granting President Johnson the authority to conduct military operations in Southeast Asia without declaring war. He was authorised:

'to take all necessary steps, including the use of armed force, to assist any member or protocol state of the Southeast Asia Collective Defense Treaty requesting assistance in defense of its freedom'.

This resolution became the legal justification for all subsequent US military activity in Vietnam. But, of course, at this time, Johnson did not believe there would be any need to escalate the war. He was convinced that the bombing of North Vietnamese territory would persuade Hanoi that it should end its support of the insurgency in the south. He also believed that the firmness of his stand against Ho Chi Minh would be beneficial to him in the November 1964 presidential election in which he faced the Republican candidate, Senator Barry Goldwater (1909-98). He was correct, winning a landslide victory and reassuring himself that the American electorate, as well as Congress, were supportive of his policies in Southeast Asia.

Escalation

In Hanoi there was little doubt that the Americans would escalate the war and, as a result, they greatly increased their preparations in the south. Even more men and weaponry were transported along the Ho Chi Minh Trail. But the south was in turmoil as sectarian violence raged between Buddhists and Catholics while politicians in

Saigon vied for power. The American embassy in Saigon struggled to persuade the competing political factions to unite and bring stability to the country. Meanwhile, there was pressure for Johnson to increase the bombing of the north, but opponents such as Under-Secretary of State George Ball pointed out that the bombing did not materially affect the insurgents in the south and, as he suggested, it might just provide Hanoi's allies – the Soviet Union and China – with the incentive to intervene and turn the conflict into a more serious war. Those who opposed this claimed that there would be an effect in the south because the morale of the South Vietnamese would be improved and it might also interrupt the flow of supplies and men from the north. Anyway, they argued, weakness on the part of the United States at this juncture would provide encouragement to the new leaders in the Kremlin and possibly the Chinese who now also had nuclear weapons. A month after being re-elected, Johnson approved a secret and much more aggressive plan that allowed for the bombing of North Vietnam. It also mentioned the probability that American ground forces would soon be fighting on Vietnamese territory.

Johnson decided to deploy troops, two US combat divisions, but it was only the beginning. By 1968, 500,000 American troops would be deployed in Vietnam. In early 1965, he was steadily increasing the bombing of targets in both North and South Vietnam. 'Sustained reprisal' bombing that enjoyed the codename 'Rolling Thunder' began in February 1965 after the Viet Cong attacked a US base at Pleiku manned by advisers. Rolling Thunder would not stop for a number of years, and 25,000 sorties were flown by US pilots in the first year alone, taking off from bases in Thailand and aircraft carriers in the Gulf of Tonkin and the South China Sea. Their targets were military bases, airfields, oil-storage facilities, supply depots and, of course, the Ho Chi Minh Trail. The number of sorties increased by more than 300 per cent the following year and by 1967 had reached 108,000. But the North Vietnamese worked together in a remarkable way to ensure the bombs did as little damage as possible and, after the raids, repairs were immediately carried out. During the raids, 600,000 of the 800,000 inhabitants of Hanoi would evacuate the city, those left behind making use of an extensive network of bunkers. Supplies were moved into the countryside, oil drums, for instance, being located in remote rural areas. Meanwhile, schools, factories and offices were re-built in areas away from the bombing. Nothing much changed, however. Goods and men still moved south and the ARVN continued to be on the receiving end of a beating from the Viet Cong, often incurring heavy casualties. In March 1965, the first American combat troops landed at Da Nang.

Meanwhile, the political turmoil in Saigon showed little sign of abating, five different governments having tried and failed since the death of Diem. The latest incumbents in the summer of 1965 were General Nguyen Van Thieu (1923-2001) and Air Marshal Nguyen Cao Ky (1930-2011) and they appeared to be no better than their predecessors. Indeed, they might even have been worse, US Assistant Secretary of State William Bundy (1917-2000) describing them as 'absolutely the bottom of the barrel'. The incompetence of both them and their army persuaded the Pentagon that it should have more control over the fighting. Consequently, General Westmoreland, supported by the Joint Chiefs of Staff, asked for the deployment of a further 150,000 US troops. For Johnson this was a crucial decision that he agonised over for a week at the end of July, seeking advice from everyone but the government of South Vietnam. The only person who was unsympathetic to Westmoreland's request was George Ball who cautioned that the decision to commit American forces in such numbers would have to result in complete victory over the DRV as falling short would seriously damage America's standing in the world. 'Our involvement will be so great,' he counselled, 'that we cannot – without national humiliation – stop short of achieving our complete objectives.' Other advisers, Robert McNamara amongst them, were of the firm belief that a substantial expansion of the US war effort, coupled with attempts to open negotiations, would finally bring a solution to the problem of Vietnam. Johnson at last reluctantly approved Westmoreland's request. 'I want war like I want polio,' he said to aides, 'but what you want and what your image is are two different things.' Nonetheless, by this time, he believed that to send more troops was the only way forward. There was no room for compromise through a diplomatic solution as that would look like a defeat for him and for the United States.

By the end of 1965, there were 184,300 US troops in South Vietnam.

Fighting the War

Johnson still insisted that the conflict in Vietnam would be only a limited war. He resisted calls, for instance, for the reserves and the National Guard to be mobilised and rejected McNamara's request that a tax be levied to help pay for the war. Meanwhile, he was diverting the public's attention away from the increasing American involvement in Vietnam with his Great Society legislation and the 'war on poverty' he claimed to be fighting. Any extension to the powers he had already been granted in the Gulf of Tonkin Resolution would have to be passed by Congress and that would give the conservative opponents to his domestic agenda the opportunity to inflict damage on it. Anyway, the means to increase military personnel was already on the statute books. America's system of conscription was based on the Selective Service System that had provided troops during the First and Second World Wars. Men over the age of eighteen could be conscripted but not everyone served. When the need for troops in Vietnam began to increase, the draft was doubled to 35,000 a month. But deferment or exemption was still possible, based on a number of criteria, including occupation, health, hardship or whether a candidate was still in the education system. 339,000 were drafted in 1966 – a rise of more than 200,000 on the previous year – more than half of whom served in Vietnam. In total, two and a half million men served in Vietnam, many enlisting voluntarily. Those who were drafted tended to be poorer and less well educated, as a result of deferment or exemption for men who were at college who tended to come from better off sections of society. Initially, although only 13 per cent of the troops that fought in Vietnam were African Americans, they represented some 20 per cent of all combat casualties, a consequence of their enlisting as a career opportunity. They chose the more dangerous combat specialities that rewarded them with higher pay. This changed after the first year of the war, as they had been part of the initial deployment before the draft. Eventually, the statistics stabilised and began to represent the racial percentages of young American men. Westmoreland called it a blue-collar war but the truth was that around 80 per cent of the young men fighting it were poor or working class.

The notion of negotiations lingered, with Johnson stating in a televised speech in April 1965 that he would accept 'unconditional discussions' and was prepared to offer the incentive of a billion-dollar development of the Mekong River Valley. 'We have made a national pledge to help South Vietnam defend its independence...', he said. 'We are also there to strengthen world order... We are also there because great stakes are in the balance... We will not withdraw.' But this was really intended for domestic consumption and for those critics who said that the bombing left little hope of a diplomatic solution. The billion-dollar offer was considered by Ho and his colleagues as little short of a bribe and a subsequent pause in the bombing in May 1965 was described by Hanoi as a 'worn out trick'. No talks were possible, they argued, while US forces remained in Vietnam. The United States responded that, until the north removed *its* troops from South Vietnam and recognised the authority of the government in Saigon, they would not withdraw a single man. Meanwhile, at the beginning of April, Johnson had quietly changed the role of the Marines in Vietnam from the static defence of base facilities to active combat patrols.

Westmoreland's strategy was one of attrition. He reasoned that his men, with their comprehensive air support and vastly superior firepower, would rack up a body count of enemy dead that would far outstrip the North's ability to replace its lost troops. The DRV, meanwhile, responded to the influx of American ground forces by sending soldiers of the regular North Vietnamese Army (NVA) along the Ho Chi Minh Trail and into South Vietnam. The first significant test for both sides came in October 1965 when the North Vietnamese launched a major offensive in the Ia Drang Valley, south of Pleiku in the Central Highlands. The US 1st Air Cavalry Division was backed up by helicopters that had the ability to move troops around rapidly and could also quickly remove casualties from the battlefield. These craft, which would become a powerful symbol of the Vietnam War, could also be used as tactical air support, as gunships. The US Air Force played a part, too, and enemy positions were bombed by tactical bombers, including the B-52. It was a battle with an unusual outcome. Battles are fought, usually, to gain territory, but as soon as the Vietnamese had departed the battlefield, so, too, did the Americans. This would become a feature of the fighting in this war; it was not about gaining territory as wars usually were. The Americans did achieve one of the objectives of Westmoreland's attritional policy, however, by killing around ten times more NVA troops than they lost. In fact, the 'body count' became the general method of calculating American progress in the war. Of course, there were major faults with this system, making it a very unreliable means of gauging success. The numbers returned to MACV were arrived at by soldiers at the scene of the fighting and with various incentives such as promotions or extra leave on offer for those who achieved the highest number of enemy kills, they were inevitably not always accurate. A more chilling aspect of this method was the number of innocent civilians – women and children included – who were killed in order to inflate the count. Naturally, this made the Americans and the South Vietnamese government even more unpopular.

Westmoreland repeatedly requested more troops and the war was now costing a huge amount of money. When it came time to put the defense budget before the House Appropriations Committee, McNamara wanted to ask for $110 billion, but was ordered by Johnson not to submit a cent more than $57 billion. Johnson remained worried that his right wing enemies in Congress would raid his Great Society budget to pay for it. The two men deviously delayed any decision on sending more troops to Vietnam until after they had approval for their budget.

There was a pause in the bombing over Christmas 1965, Johnson responding to critics in the media and in Congress who once again said that no opportunity was being given for a negotiated solution. Representatives of Britain and Poland were contacted, those two countries having offered to act as intermediaries in any discussions between the DRV and the United States. But there was also criticism from the more hawkish members of the government and from the military who believed, as Admiral U.S. Grant Sharp Jr. (1906-2001) said, that the combat forces in Vietnam were being 'required to fight the war with one hand tied behind their backs.' As Johnson had expected, nothing happened on the diplomatic front and Rolling Thunder was resumed on 31 January.

No Further Forward

One of the problems of the Vietnam War for the Americans was defining what victory would look like. They faced an enemy that disappeared into the night and replaced its dead with even more men determined to sacrifice their lives for their country. A year after the first American marines had landed at Da Nang, there were 267,500 American troops in Vietnam, a number rising to 385,000 by the end of the year, but there was little to show that could be defined as success or even progress. Johnson put pressure on his own commanders and on the South Vietnamese leaders President Nguyen Van Thieu and Prime Minister Nguyen Cao Ky whom he met twice in 1966, at Honolulu in February and Manila in October. He was reassured, especially by Westmoreland, that things were moving in the right direction. Attrition continued, with search-and-destroy operations that added to that all-important body count, but the NLF continued to control large parts of the country and the Ho Chi Minh Trail was still supplying them with men and equipment. Defense Secretary McNamara was privately beginning to have doubts that the war would end any time soon, thoughts that he shared with the President, counselling him to seek talks with Hanoi. In November, however, Poland offered to help initiate negotiations. The codename Marigold was given to this diplomatic initiative that would involve the USA suspending bombing and the North Vietnamese suspending its infiltration of South Vietnam. These tentative efforts to find a diplomatic solution ended when the US Air Force conducted an air strike in the vicinity of Hanoi on 2 December, the Americans claiming that the bombing had actually been stopped by the weather conditions and had nothing to do with the Polish diplomatic efforts. In the coming months there were further tentative attempts. The US State Department tried to contact North Vietnamese diplomats in Moscow and, on 8 February 1967, Johnson sent a private message to Ho Chi Minh suggesting discussions between their representatives. He again insisted that the United States would only stop the bombing when Ho stopped infiltrating the south. For his part, the North Vietnamese leader responded by criticising American aggression and let Johnson know that 'the Vietnamese people will never yield to force nor agree to talks under the menace of bombs.' (Gary R. Hess, *Presidential Decisions for War: Korea, Vietnam and the Persian Gulf* Baltimore, MD: Johns Hopkins University Press, 2001).

Meanwhile, Westmoreland had been planning a new strategy to enhance his attritional approach to the fighting, introducing large unit search-and-destroy operations. The ARVN took over the tasks of occupation, pacification and security, freeing American troops to patrol rural areas in large numbers, sometimes tens of thousands. Operations codenamed Cedar Falls and Junction City were launched in the Iron Triangle, an area north and west of the southern capital. They were relentless and ruthless initiatives. MACV declared certain areas, believed to be under NLF control, to be 'free-strike zones' and these were subjected to carpet-bombing by B-52s, artillery fire and the spraying of chemical defoliants that destroyed vegetation as well as crops. Entire villages were wiped from the face of the earth, resulting in a desperate need for refugee camps that were soon filled with unhappy and downright hostile people. As ever, however, the Viet Cong merely dissolved into the jungle and waited for the Americans to move on before returning to re-establish control of whatever villages had been left standing. Of course, the bombing of the 'free-strike zones' provided Ho with marvellous propaganda that he could use to bolster his people's spirit and to demonstrate that the Americans cared little for the people they were supposed to be freeing.

Ho's strategy in the war was little different to that used against the French. 'Protracted war' Hanoi called it and it involved simply avoiding the large-scale, fixed battles that would give the Americans the opportunity to exploit their technological superiority. It was a policy of harassment in which PAVN and NLF units would ambush American troops, plant cunningly designed booby traps and fire on them from temporary positions from which they could evacuate and disappear at any moment. They hoped that this protracted warfare would eventually persuade the American government that the war was, effectively, unwinnable and that the political will to continue would disappear.

Supplying the DRV

Meanwhile, the North Vietnamese war effort was being supported in no small way by Moscow and Beijing. For Moscow, it was, despite Premier Nikita Khrushchev's (1894-1971) insistence on the Soviet Union supporting wars of national liberation, as much a matter of international credibility as it was for the United States. The Soviets had initially been hesitant in their support for the DRV, reluctant to risk a confrontation with America but they still provided a huge amount of vital equipment, including telecommunications equipment, vehicles and medicines. Vietnam's surface-to-air missiles (SAMs), vital in their efforts to combat the Rolling Thunder bombing raids, were Russian and the Soviet Union also sent them fighter planes, anti-aircraft guns and radar equipment, together with advisers to teach them how to use this equipment. Many PAVN troops received training in the Soviet Union.

China had, of course, long been a hated enemy of the Vietnamese, but since seizing power, the Chinese communist government had enjoyed good relations with Hanoi, recognising the DRV as the government of Vietnam and it had provided aid and advice in the war against the French. Following the Gulf of Tonkin incident, China had been quick to issue a statement condemning what it called 'US imperialist aggression against Vietnam'. Chinese leader Mao Zedong was at the time attempting to bring more radical thinking back to his country, the subsequent Cultural Revolution being a manifestation of this, but he was also anxious to make the Soviet Union look bad. In meetings that Vietnamese leaders had with top Chinese officials, including Premier Zhou Enlai (1898-1976), General Luo Ruiqing (1906-78) and Chairman Mao himself, it was made clear to the Vietnamese that, should the United States invade North Vietnam, China would not hesitate to send in its forces. During the subsequent four years they dispatched 320,000 anti-aircraft and engineering troops to North Vietnam. These specialist soldiers helped in the re-building of bomb-damaged roads and bridges, for example. Johnson, anxious to avoid confrontation with China or the Soviet Union, ensured that bombing raids did not target their troops.

Pacification and McNamara Begins to Doubt

As 1967 dawned, there was little change. Diplomatic initiatives in the early part of the year involving Soviet Premier Kosygin and British Prime Minister Harold Wilson came to nothing, Westmoreland's large-unit offensive in the Iron Triangle had not dented the will of Hanoi and there was increased public protest and criticism of the American war effort in the United States. Johnson now began to focus on pacification, emphasising this to the South Vietnamese leaders when he met them in Guam in March 1967. He returned to his plan to develop the Mekong Delta and created an initiative directed at pacification – Civilian Operations and Revolutionary Development Support (CORDS). It was headed by a member of his staff, Robert Comer (1922-2000), who was also appointed civilian deputy commander of MACV. The aim of CORDS was to win the hearts and minds of the disaffected rural South Vietnamese through economic and social development initiatives. These included refugee resettlement, efforts to improve public health, and the Chieu Hoi programme – a scheme to persuade Viet Cong to defect.

This was all anathema to Westmoreland who believed that pacification would take another decade. He was convinced he could win a military victory using search-and-destroy tactics if he had more troops and, to this end, requested a further 200,000. McNamara was unconvinced and warned Johnson in a memo on 19 May that sending even more troops to Vietnam could prove to be 'a national disaster'. He explained that Ho Chi Minh could easily match whatever numbers the USA sent and that the war, was, therefore, in a state of stalemate. He further recommended that the bombing of the north be scaled down. Stopping the bombing, he argued, would show the world that it was not the United States that was blocking the way to peace. Pacification and diplomatic efforts should be continued, he advised. He ended the memo with the words:

'The picture of the world's greatest superpower killing or injuring more than 1,000 non-combatants a month while trying to pound a tiny backward nation into submission on an issue whose merits are hotly disputed is not a pretty one.'

But Johnson remained unmoved, having been persuaded by the JCS to keep up the unrelenting pressure on Hanoi. Westmoreland did not get the number of troops he asked for, however. Johnson approved only 55,000. McNamara did not give up. On 1 November, another long memo arrived in the presidential in-tray. Now the Secretary of Defense was recommending a complete change of direction. His proposal was aimed at what he termed 'stabilisation'. Firstly, he again proposed no increase in troop levels and a halt to bombing. He recommended the introduction of strategies that would lead to a reduction in American casualties, would give the government of South Vietnam greater responsibility for the security of its country and achieve a reduction in the damage being done to the 'people and wealth of South Vietnam'.

As with his previous memo, Johnson declined to respond directly. Instead, he showed it to various people, including Secretary of State Dean Rusk and his national security adviser, Walt Rostow. With the author of the memo being kept anonymous, Rostow was tasked with showing it to other advisers. Eventually, on 2 November, Johnson called a meeting of the group known as the 'Wise Men', an unofficial collective of foreign policy advisers that included, as well as McNamara and Rusk, General Maxwell Taylor, US Supreme Court Justice Abe Fortas (1910-82), Clark Clifford (1906-98), George Ball, McGeorge Bundy (1919-96), General Omar Bradley

(1893-1981), Henry Cabot Lodge, Dean Acheson (1893-1971), CIA Director Richard Helms (1913-2002) and Assistant Secretary of State William Bundy. The meeting went well for Johnson. Astonishingly, some such as Clark Clifford, even described the war as 'an enormous success' and claimed that continued pressure would wear down the North Vietnamese will to continue. To follow McNamara's plan, he suggested, would be disastrous:

> 'The chortles of unholy glee issuing from Hanoi would be audible in every capital of the world. Is this evidence of our zeal and courage to stay the course? Of course not! It would be interpreted to be exactly what it is. A resigned and discouraged effort to find a way out of a conflict for which we had lost our will and dedication.'

Gibbons, William Conrad, *The U. S. Government and the Vietnam War: Executive and Legislative Roles and Relationships*, Princeton University Press, Princeton, 2014

Regarding the negative perception of the war in the media, Rostow claimed that it should be possible to guide the press so that they would show the war in a more positive light and that they could be convinced that the end was in sight. Amazingly, Johnson was able to leave the meeting with approval for his conduct of the war. He had at no time mentioned McNamara's memorandum or even asked for his opinion of the status of the conflict. McNamara later wrote that 'the Wise Men had no clue that all this was going on'. It was another example of the obfuscation practised by the Johnson White House. Rostow, for instance, had asked CIA Vietnam analyst George Allen to provide him with an intelligence summary that would convince congressmen and White House visitors in the coming weeks that all was well with the pacification programme. Allen refused.

Summoned to Washington to deliver a progress report in

November 1967, General Westmoreland announced that a turning point had been reached in the war. The North Vietnamese were now losing more men than they could replace, he claimed. 'We have reached an important point,' he said, 'when the end begins to come into view.' How true was this? Not very, is the answer. Indeed, Viet Cong losses were huge – three times those of the United States and ARVN forces since the war had effectively begun in 1965 – but against this should have been placed the knowledge that there were now more North Vietnamese troops in South Vietnam than ever and that the NLF was still in control in many areas of the south. Meanwhile in Saigon Buddhist protests continued and politicians and officials were more interested in lining their pockets than winning the war. There were now 485,000 American troops in South Vietnam and they were making not a jot of difference.

Anti-War Protests

As American commitment to Vietnam increased, so, too, did opposition to the war. Public opinion had initially been favourable towards it but, as time went on, a highly vocal, spontaneous protest movement developed. Unlike the civil rights movement that had Dr Martin Luther King (1929-68), it had no figurehead and there was no overall organising body. Instead it was made up of a collection of pacifists, anti-imperialists, peace liberals and ordinary people. Thousands took part in a variety of ways – mass demonstrations, rallies where draftees would burn their draft cards, lobbying of politicians and violent protest. Most protesters were young and more often than not students, but older people also became involved and even Vietnam veterans protested against the war. The problem they faced was that the media focused on their more radical elements which led to them being viewed as something of a fringe movement when, in reality, many ordinary people, young and old, were engaged in the protests. They also lacked organisation and a unified objective, which did not help in getting their message across coherently. Some wanted complete withdrawal from Vietnam while others demanded a negotiated settlement. There were numerous notable incidents. The famous paediatrician, Dr Benjamin Spock (1903-98), had in the 1950s been a member of SANE, an organisation that campaigned against nuclear weapons, and he re-emerged with a series of public letters that protested about the war. In March 1965, an 82-year-old woman, Alice Herz (1882-1965), a member of another 1950s organisation, Women Strike for Peace, shockingly burned herself to death in Detroit, a terrible recreation of the desperate acts of Buddhist monks in Saigon in the early 1960s. Teachers at the University of Michigan staged an event called a 'teach-in' in tribute to her, an attempt to inform students and the public about what was going on in Vietnam. Other universities followed suit and famous people such as the writer Norman Mailer (1923-2007) took part in massively attended events. 20,000 people turned up for a protest in Washington DC on 17 April, organised by Students for a Democratic Society (SDS) and there were further protests in the coming months. Demonstrators in Manhattan on 16 October faced counter-demonstrators who declared the marchers to be communists. However, the 27 November march in Washington DC by 35,000 people of all ages, organised by SANE, was a protest of a different order. Coretta Scott King (1927-2006), wife of Martin Luther King, Carl Oglesby (1935-2011), President of the SDS and Dr Spock all took the podium to speak that day.

Unfortunately for the anti-war protesters, the more sensational New York protest received more coverage and helped to highlight the quandary in which the movement found itself. There was little doubt that many ordinary Americans – not all young and not all hippies – were turning against American involvement in Vietnam, but the radical element of the protests made for good television and it was those elements that were appearing in the media, creating the perception, therefore, that anti-war protesters were extremists.

Incidents continued and, horrifically, two more people protested the war by setting themselves on fire. One of them, Norman Morrison (1933-65), a 31-year-old pacifist, self-immolated beneath the window of Robert McNamara's office at the Pentagon.

In 1966, the Fulbright Hearings began, a series of televised US Senate Foreign Relations Committee hearings, chaired by Democratic Senator J. William Fulbright (1905-95) of Arkansas. Running until 1971, these hearings included testimony from both supporters and opponents of the war. Nothing changed as a result, but as they proceeded, they lent the anti-war movement more credibility. However, in the congressional elections held at the end of the year, domestic issues such as Johnson's Great Society were still more likely to be debated than the war in Indochina. Indeed, a Gallup poll in 1966 showed 59 per cent of Americans still believing that sending troops to Vietnam was the right thing to do. The anti-war movement was dramatically brought into focus as the World Heavyweight Boxing champion, Muhammad Ali (born 1942) – formerly Cassius Clay – announced that he was a conscientious objector, famously saying, 'Man, I ain't got no quarrel with them Viet Cong'. When drafted, he refused to go to Vietnam, sensationally receiving a five-year prison sentence for draft evasion, a conviction that was overturned on appeal.

1967 saw the American public become weary of the war, especially as more than 11,000 American servicemen had lost their lives in Vietnam by the end of the year. Protests continued. A 'Human Be-In' at Golden Gate Park in San Francisco in January 1967 attracted around 30,000 people; in March a three-page anti-war advert appeared in *The New York Times* bearing the names of 6,766 teachers, lecturers and professors; the same month, Dr Martin Luther King led 5,000 in an anti-war march in Chicago; in April, 100,000 marched in San Francisco and, the same day, 400,000 joined a march from Central Park to the United Nations building in New York, organised by the National Mobilization Committee to

End the War in Vietnam. The same committee organised a march of 100,000 on the Pentagon on 21 October. There were violent clashes as protesters tried to breach police lines, but there were also bizarre antics such as the attempt by some, including poet Allen Ginsberg (1926-97) and political activists Jerry Rubin (1938-94) and Abbie Hoffman (1936-89), to exorcise and levitate the Pentagon building. Flowers that were going to be dropped from a plane onto the Pentagon were instead stuck in the barrels of the rifles of Military Policemen, providing some of the most powerful images of the anti-war movement. The chant on this occasion, as at many other protests during those years, was the chilling 'Hey, Hey, LBJ! How many kids did you kill today?'

For Johnson the increasing protest was, of course, deeply troubling. It not only disturbed public order and threatened his political status and credibility, he and his advisers also worried about the effect it would have on Hanoi. They feared that it would provide encouragement to Ho Chi Minh and his countrymen to continue to resist peace negotiations until the American people themselves forced Johnson to withdraw American troops from Vietnam. Johnson was, himself, incredulous about the protesters, believing that Americans would not behave this way and began to believe that communists were behind the protest movement. He even ordered the CIA and the FBI to undertake investigations, but they could not come up with anything to prove that any outside interests were being brought to bear on the movement.

The two opposing camps in America were labelled on the one side 'hawks' – those who pushed for America to continue the war to its conclusion which, they argued, should be brought about by more bombing and an increase in the deployment of troops – and 'doves' on the other – those who wanted an end to American involvement in Indochina at any cost, even if that meant making compromises that might make it look to the rest of the world as if Hanoi had won. Towards the end of 1967, however, despite bombing pauses designed to encourage negotiations, there was little change in the attitudes of the Americans and the North Vietnamese. Johnson, General Westmoreland and others made efforts to convince the American public that Westmoreland's approach was working and that the end was in sight. 'The ranks of the Viet Cong are thinning steadily,' said the general at a banquet at the White House. And at a National Press Club event, he assured the audience, 'We have reached an important point when the end begins to come into view... It is significant that the enemy has not won a major battle in more than a year. In general, he can fight his large forces only at the edges of his sanctuaries... His guerrilla force is declining at a steady rate.' He seemed even more bullish when talking to a *Time* interviewer, 'I hope they try something because we are looking for a fight.' The interviewer would have done well to remind him of the old saying, 'Be careful what you wish for.'

The Tet Offensive

In July 1967, senior North Vietnamese diplomats were recalled from around the world for meetings with Ho Chi Minh, General Giap and other members of the government. The outcome of these consultations was a decision to change the nature of the war. North Vietnam would, for the first time, launch a full-scale military offensive aimed at creating the 'utmost confusion' amongst the Americans and the South Vietnamese government. Viet Cong and PAVN troops would attack towns and cities throughout the south and the underground network of communist operatives would rise up and, with the help of South Vietnamese sympathisers, seize local government, bringing down the hated regime headed by Thieu and Ky in Saigon. The leaders in Hanoi were perfectly aware of the growing unease about the war in America. They believed that a disastrous defeat in an election year could do untold damage to the American cause at home and bring their exit from Vietnam closer.

A decisive victory would also put Hanoi in a powerful position to go to the negotiating table.

To learn how to gain maximum surprise with the offensive, Ho and his colleagues looked back through Vietnamese history to 1789 when the army of the Tay Son Montagnards attacked Chinese troops who were at the time occupying Hanoi. Victory on that occasion was achieved by launching the attack at the most unexpected moment – during the sacred holiday of Tet, the Vietnamese New Year. Tet is the cultural event of the year in Vietnam, celebrated with special holiday foods, visits to neighbours and family and worship at temples. In autumn 1967, as was customary, the North Vietnamese declared they would observe a truce from 27 January until 3 February. This year, however, they had no intention of observing it. The South Vietnamese eagerly took advantage of the situation, granting leave to many troops against the advice of General Westmoreland and MACV, although, fortunately, the general managed to persuade Thieu to ensure that at least 50 per cent of ARVN troops would remain on duty over the holiday. Westmoreland worried that something was afoot, a concern increased by the capture of some Viet Cong carrying pre-recorded audiotapes appealing to people to rise up. Still, however, there was no panic amongst the Americans and South Vietnamese. Thieu left Saigon to spend the holiday with his wife's family in My Tho in the Mekong Delta as South Vietnam wound down for the holiday.

Despite all the careful planning in Hanoi, for reasons that remain a mystery, some North Vietnamese troops attacked twenty-four hours early. Before daylight on 30 January 1968, eight towns and cities in the Central Highlands and in the central coastal provinces came under attack. Amongst their targets was Da Nang, home to the headquarters of the ARVN's 1 Corps which was struck by PAVN commandos, known to the Americans as 'sappers', while attacks were also launched on Pleiku, Qui Nhon and other places. It was a useful indication to the Americans of what was about to happen and Major General Philip B. Davidson (1915-96), Westmoreland's chief of intelligence, gravely warned: 'This is going to happen in the rest of the country tonight and tomorrow morning.' It was enough for President Thieu to cancel the ceasefire and put his troops on alert but it was too late for him to be able to recall all those troops already on leave. Meanwhile, South Vietnamese towns and cities were swarming with PAVN troops in civilian clothing who had infiltrated the south along the Ho Chi Minh Trail in recent months and now awaited their moment.

It came shortly after midnight on 30 January, when 84,000 Viet Cong, sometimes with the support of PAVN troops, attacked more than a hundred towns, cities and hamlets, including Saigon. This was a complete change of strategy. Previously, they had focused on the Vietnamese countryside but now they were re-directing that focus onto South Vietnam's urban areas. Before the attack they received an exhortation from Hanoi: 'Crack the Sky, Shake the Earth', and were told that they were 'about to inaugurate the greatest battle in the history of our country'. The attacks followed a similar pattern in every case – mortar and/or rocket bombardments followed by massed assaults by battalion-strength ground forces. Local operatives provided intelligence and guides. They unsuccessfully attacked Nha Trang on the coast and followed that with assaults on coastal areas that had previously been beyond their reach. Cam Ranh Air Base, a large US facility where US military personnel entered or left Vietnam, was hit. Highland towns were attacked and sixteen provincial capitals in the Mekong Delta were overrun. The Viet Cong fought relentlessly, sometimes abandoning their customarily flexible tactics to defend positions that were frankly untenable. The brutality of their attacks was frightening and many minor government officials, foreign doctors, teachers and missionaries were murdered. They even attacked the Saigon region, the US embassy in the centre of the capital being a prime target. Nineteen Viet Cong commandos blasted a hole in the wall of the embassy and killed five US troops, television pictures of the assault being beamed into millions of American living rooms. The scale of the attacks left American officials dazed but Westmoreland appeared confident and unruffled on television, telling reporters that the Communists had been deceitful in breaking the truce. He assured them that their 'well-laid plans went afoul' but inside he was deeply rattled and the US public was shocked by the sight of bodies inside the embassy compound. They watched as skirmishes erupted across Saigon live on their TV screens. One of the most iconic images of this First Battle of Saigon, and, indeed, of the whole war, occurred the next day on a street in the city when General Nguyen Ngoc Loan (1930-98) executed a captive Viet Cong with a bullet to the head, all captured on film by an NBC cameraman and Associated Press photographer, Eddie Adams (1933–2004). It was greeted with horror by the American public and the world.

Meanwhile, one of the bloodiest battles of the entire war was being fought in the old royal city of Hue. About 7,500 Communists attacked the city from three directions early on the morning of 31 January, the South Vietnamese garrison putting up little resistance. The Viet Cong then slaughtered government functionaries, police officers and anyone connected with the South Vietnamese government, and many foreigners, shooting them, clubbing them to death or burying them alive. Around 3,000 people died. US troops were forced to clear out the enemy street by street and, often, house by house, television crews following hard on their heels, filming for transmission to American living rooms. Throughout February, the Americans and the South Vietnamese army fought their way towards the Citadel in the centre of the city and, on 24 February, Hue was finally back in the hands of US and ARVN forces.

In early March, MACV reported that since the launch of the Tet Offensive, 2,000 American and 4,000 ARVN troops had lost their lives while they estimated that around 50,000 Viet Cong had died. Such huge losses were decisive for the Viet Cong, finishing them as a fighting force and, for the remainder of the war, the majority of operations were carried out by the PAVN. But the initial assaults had been successful, especially as the North Vietnamese had staged border battles at Song Be, Lok Ninh and Dak To and had created diversions by building up forces around the Khe Sanh Combat Base and other facilities in remote areas. This forced MACV to divert troops away from cities and towns, the real targets of the Tet Offensive. But the main part of Tet was over and it was undoubtedly a military defeat for the communists. However, the effect it had on the US government and the shock it caused to the American public, glued to the scenes of fighting on their television screens, was profound. Many Americans perceived Tet as a defeat and certain evidence that, contrary to what they were being told, there was still a long way to go in the war. They had, after all, been led to believe by their politicians and generals that the North Vietnamese and the Viet Cong were incapable of such a devastating assault. As PAVN General Tran Do (1924-2002) later said:

'In all honesty, we didn't achieve our main objective, which was to spur uprisings across the south. Still, we inflicted heavy casualties on the Americans and their puppets, and that was a big gain for us. As for making an impact on the United States, it had not been our intention – but it turned out to be a fortunate result.'

The media were disparaging about the war effort and ever more distrustful of official updates. One of the most respected American media figures, Walter Cronkite (1916-2009), broadcast a special report while the Tet Offensive was in progress, famously announcing:

'To say that we are mired in stalemate seems the only realistic, yet unsatisfactory, conclusion... it is increasingly clear to this reporter

that the only rational way out then will be to negotiate, not as
victors, but as an honorable people who lived up to their pledge to
defend democracy, and did the best they could.'

On being told of Cronkite's remarks, President Johnson is reported
to have complained: 'If I've lost Cronkite, I've lost Middle America'.
Newsmen now began to bring up Johnson's optimism of the previous
autumn. There had even been predictions of US troop withdrawals
starting in 1969. This now looked like a distant possibility to the
media, even though withdrawals did actually begin that year. The Tet
Offensive was presented to the American people on television and
in newspapers as an unmitigated disaster, even a defeat, although it
had manifestly been a victory. Perhaps Johnson and the members of
his government were now paying the price for their recent economy
with the truth.

It was clear to all that many more American lives would be lost in
Vietnam before the war was over and Tet was the last straw for many
who were now firmly of the belief that the United States should
remove its forces from Indochina as quickly as possible. Of course,
there were those who saw it differently, considering such remarks
as Cronkite's and similarly pessimistic reporting to be a betrayal of
the nation. After all, they argued, with Tet the communists had not
achieved their objectives and it had been a military victory for the
Americans and South Vietnamese that had somehow been turned
into a psychological defeat.

It mattered little, because from this point on it was unlikely that
it was going to end well for America. Tet had clearly demonstrated
that the US strategy was not working. The sheer numbers involved
from the North Vietnamese side in the offensive and the volume of
equipment they had were clear evidence of the American failure
to stop men and supplies being infiltrated into the south in great
numbers and quantities. That would not cease as the PAVN sought
to replace the Viet Cong troops who had not survived Tet. It was a

seemingly limitless supply and simply bore out the warning of Ho Chi Minh to the French when he was fighting them: 'You can kill ten of my men for every one I kill of yours. But, even at those odds, you will lose and I will win'.

More Offensives and 'Mini-Tet'

Fighting continued, even as the North Vietnamese agreed to attend peace negotiations in Paris, each side convinced that the other was in a weakened state. 42 US and 37 ARVN battalions spent March and April clearing the Viet Cong out of the area around Saigon but in late April, to increase their bargaining position at the peace talks, the North Vietnamese launched another offensive. By this time, they had flooded troops down the Ho Chi Minh Trail to take the places of those they had lost during Tet. The US logistical base at Dong Ha, the most northerly town in South Vietnam, saw prolonged combat throughout May, 8,000 troops of the PAVN attacking with the support of artillery fired from across the Demilitarized Zone. This vicious struggle, in which the PAVN clashed with US marines as well as ARVN troops, became known as the Battle of Dai Do. More than 2,000 PAVN troops perished and the Americans and South Vietnamese lost 290 killed, with almost 1,000 wounded. This was followed by another North Vietnamese offensive, dubbed 'Mini-Tet' by the Americans and South Vietnamese. Communist units attacked 119 targets in South Vietnam, again including Saigon. This time, however, they lacked the element of surprise and many were intercepted before reaching their objectives. Some did succeed in penetrating the cordon around the capital, however, and there was heavy fighting. In the district of Phu Lam, it took several days to deal with troops of the 267th Viet Cong Local Force Battalion and hard combat took place in other districts of the city. By the time the North Vietnamese withdrew, on 12 May, they had suffered heavy casualties, including around 3,000 dead. At Kham Duc, a Special Forces observation camp, the Americans suffered one of their worst setbacks of the war. This remote base, further south than Dong Ha, was accessible only by air. When it came under intense attack by two regiments of the 2nd PAVN Division, MACV took the decision to abandon it. Its 1,800 US and ARVN troops were evacuated by air under constant heavy fire. Despite yet again suffering heavy losses, the PAVN took control of this vital surveillance base close to the Laotian border. On 25 May, there were further attacks on Saigon, and the communists this time occupied six Buddhist temples, erroneously believing that the allies would be reluctant to use artillery or air power against such buildings. The action was again disastrous for the inhabitants of Saigon, 87,000 rendered homeless by the fighting and 500 losing their lives. This phase of the war took 161 American lives with almost 4,000 wounded.

In the summer months of 1968, the US 7th Cavalry and the 101st Airborne were helicoptered into the A Shau Valley. Located to the west of the city of Hue, close to the border with Laos, the valley served as a base for large numbers of PAVN who slipped back over the border into Laos before much damage could be done to them. The North Korean offensive picked up again on 17 August, attacks on towns close to the border – Tay Ninh, An Loc and Loc Ninh – preceding it and acting as diversionary targets aimed at drawing forces away from the real targets. Again, Saigon was attacked but this time the communists were more easily defeated. MACV judged this offensive 'a dismal failure' and claimed that, in the five weeks of its duration, 20,000 North Vietnamese troops died while the United States lost 700.

1968 was, indeed, a bloody year. 16,899 American troops were killed – the highest annual tally of the war so far – and 150,000 were wounded. The North Vietnamese leadership was dismayed by the failure of their various offensives and their loss of life was huge.

Somewhere between 85,000 and 100,000 of their troops had taken part in the 'Border Battles' of 1967 and the 1968 winter-spring campaign. Of these 45,267 had died.

There was complete turmoil in South Vietnam during and after the Tet Offensive. With government troops pulled back to defend the cities and towns, the countryside was wide open for the communists to seize control, which they did, bringing a halt to the US pacification programmes. Their objective had been to destabilise the Saigon government and that, at least, had been achieved. Even with the support of the Americans, the government, it seemed, was incapable of protecting its own people. This was evident from some of the statistics. It was estimated that there had been 14,300 civilian deaths and 24,000 civilians had been wounded. The refugee problem had become critical, with 630,000 joining the 800,000 that the war had already created. One in twelve South Vietnamese was living in a refugee camp. The ARVN, too, had its problems. During 1968, desertion rates escalated from 10.5 per thousand to 16.5 per thousand, possibly as a result of the high casualty rate – 27,915 of its soldiers had been killed during the year.

Manoeuvring in Washington

The question for Johnson was whether he could ever win in Vietnam fighting his 'limited' war. Many argued that it could never be won with the number of troops that were there at the time. This was put into sharp focus when General Earle Wheeler (1908-75), chair of the Joint Chiefs of Staff, encouraged General Westmoreland to put in a request for more troops. On 11 February 1968, Wheeler argued with Johnson that acquiescing to Westmoreland's request would allow him to regain the initiative after the nightmare of Tet and even to go on the offensive when the time was right. Westmoreland consequently asked for more men. The real game that was in play, however, concerned American reservists that the

JCS had long wanted to be called up. Wheeler pointed out, when passing Westmoreland's request to Johnson, that when the new, additional troops were dispatched to Vietnam, they would leave the total United States armed forces seriously depleted. Army units in Europe had lost officers and non-commissioned officers to Vietnam and the only combat-ready division defending the United States was the 82nd Airborne and even that had lost a third of its number to Indochina. This could only be remedied by calling up 100,000 army and marine reservists. Johnson was, naturally, reluctant to take such a step, knowing it would not go down well with public opinion. It would also cost an extraordinary amount of money. The idea was sidelined but Westmoreland responded by presenting an analysis of the situation that argued in favour of a larger deployment of new troops. He claimed that the war had changed. Instead of fighting a protracted war, he maintained that the North Vietnamese were now aiming to achieve a swift victory. This effort was proving very costly to them in terms of casualties and there was an opportunity to exploit this situation and bring the conflict to a rapid conclusion.

Wheeler flew to Vietnam on 23 February, where he persuaded Westmoreland that things were about to change in Washington. McNamara was to be replaced by the more hawkish Clark Clifford (1906-98) and it was likely that Johnson would approve attacks by US ground troops on communist strongholds in Cambodia and Laos. He suggested to Westmoreland, therefore, that he should submit a huge troop increase to cover these eventualities. Returning to Washington, the wily Wheeler mentioned none of this in connection with Westmoreland's request. Rather, he said, Westmoreland was in a perilous situation and, if the extra troops were not forthcoming, he could face serious problems. Wheeler's words were very concerning to Clifford and Johnson who, according to Clifford, was 'as worried as I have ever seen him'.

Johnson assembled a group on 28 February – it became known as the 'Clifford Group' – to both evaluate Westmoreland's request and to provide a comprehensive re-assessment of American policy in Indochina. The usual arguments were put forward, some suggesting that with more troops the war could be won militarily and others reminding them that the North Vietnamese had limitless numbers of troops willing to be sacrificed. The bombing should be stopped, the latter group argued, and everything should be directed towards reaching a negotiated settlement. The final report that was delivered on 4 March seemed to suggest, however, that US policy should continue more or less as before. It suggested that increasing troop numbers would not bring the conflict to an end and would entail 'substantial costs'. There would be the risk of diverting funds at home from social and economic development into military expenditure, thus creating the possibility of 'a domestic crisis of unprecedented proportions'. It was proposed that American troops in South Vietnam be diverted to patrolling populated areas along the coast and that the ARVN be trained and equipped sufficiently to increase its effectiveness.

The US Department of Defense's history of US involvement in Vietnam – known as the 'Pentagon Papers' – describes the quandary in which Johnson and his advisers now found themselves:

'A fork in the road had been reached and the alternatives stood out in stark reality... To deny [Wheeler's request for more troops], or to attempt to cut it to a size which could be sustained by the thinly stretched active forces, would just as surely signify that an upper limit to the U.S. military commitment in South Vietnam had been reached.'

The request for more troops was leaked to the *New York Times* and the article that followed on 10 March also spoke of the policy re-assessment that was being undertaken. The headline read: 'WESTMORELAND REQUESTS 206,000 MORE MEN, STIRRING DEBATE IN ADMINISTRATION'. The question this begged, obviously, was this: if US troops had inflicted such a severe defeat on the PAVN, why on earth were so many more needed?

By this time, McNamara had been replaced by the well-connected Clifford who had consistently supported Johnson's policy in Vietnam. The president hoped he would provide him with steadier support than he had enjoyed from the previous incumbent. Although Clifford continued to espouse a hard and hawkish line in public, however, in his own mind doubts were beginning to emerge. Following a tour of America's allies in late summer 1967, he had begun to wonder whether America's analysis of the threat communism posed to Southeast Asia had, possibly, been somewhat exaggerated. By 1 March, when he moved into McNamara's office in the Pentagon, he was even more concerned about America's role in Vietnam and the manner in which the war was being presented by the generals. A military solution seemed increasingly unlikely, he concluded; de-escalation was the only option.

Although opposition to the war was mounting amongst the press and business leaders and the media were beginning to voice concerns about the drain on the national economy, at least the polls had been giving Johnson some good news. In January 1968, a Gallup poll showed that 58 per cent of people questioned considered themselves to be 'hawks' on the question of Vietnam, while 27 per cent characterised themselves as 'doves'. After the launch of Tet, 61 per cent called themselves 'hawks' while 23 per cent preferred to call themselves 'doves', 16 per cent having no opinion. But Johnson's performance during the offensive undoubtedly damaged him. He made few comments at the time and seemed to the American public to be uncertain and indecisive. By the end of February, his personal approval rating had plummeted from 63 to 47 per cent.

The president was now very worried about the cost of the additional troops – 5 to 7 billion dollars – and the renewed danger that his Great Society programme would be raided for it. On 24 March, he announced that only 13,500 extra troops would be sent to Vietnam, far below Wheeler's requested number. On 26 March, he called together his council of Wise Men but the men in the room were in a very different mood to the last time they had met, just a few months ago in November. Then, with a couple of exceptions, they had been hawkish in the extreme about the war. Shocked the night before this meeting by a briefing on the current situation by General William DePuy (1919-92), CIA analyst George Carver (1930-94) and Ambassador to South Vietnam Philip Habib (1920-92), all but four of them called for America to withdraw from Southeast Asia. Dean Acheson (1893-1971), Secretary of State during Harry Truman's presidency, gloomily said: 'We can no longer do the job we set out to do in the time we have left and we must begin to take steps to disengage.' Johnson was bemused and asked for the same briefing that the Wise Men had received but he failed to understand why they had come to such a pessimistic conclusion because, to his mind, the war was not lost and there were still other options to explore, both military and diplomatic. The fact remained, however, that to continue in the current manner would be costly and was unlikely to move the situation on from the stalemate that currently prevailed.

Exit Johnson

The first primary to find the Democratic candidate for the 1968 presidential election took place in New Hampshire. Up to that point, Johnson had succeeded in preventing Vietnam from becoming a domestic political issue, gaining support from both sides of the House for his actions and marginalising opponents to the war by labelling them as extremists and radicals. One of his principal opponents for the nomination was Minnesota Senator Eugene McCarthy (1916-2005) who aimed to make Vietnam the central focus of his bid for the nomination. It did not look promising for McCarthy, however, and polls in February showed him achieving only 20 per cent of the Democratic vote in New Hampshire.

With Johnson yet to announce his candidature, his name was not on the ballot, but Johnson activists had organised a write-in vote where his name could be added to the ballot paper by voters. The Johnson adverts read: 'The Communists in Vietnam are watching the New Hampshire primary'. If they were watching, they would have been as surprised as everyone else by the result. Johnson won, as expected, but Senator McCarthy was a mere 300 votes behind him. It looked at the time like a decisively anti-war vote but later research indicated that the voters of New Hampshire were probably displaying their unhappiness with the Johnson administration in general, as opposed to simply voting against the war. A few days later, New York Senator Robert Kennedy (1925-68), brother of the late President Kennedy, announced his candidacy and let it be known that in his campaign he would exploit Johnson's handling of the war. The president, meanwhile, was defiant in his speeches. 'The time has come when we ought to stand up and be counted,' he told a gathering of farmers in Minneapolis, 'when we ought to support our leaders, our government, our men and our allies until aggression is stopped, wherever it has occurred.' The Wisconsin primary, scheduled for 2 April and featuring both Robert Kennedy and Eugene McCarthy on the ballot paper, was expected to be a black day for Lyndon Johnson.

Johnson was scheduled to broadcast to the nation on 31 March and it would be one of the most dramatic presidential broadcasts ever shown. A haggard, sunken-eyed president appeared on America's television screens that night to tell them that he wanted to talk about peace in Vietnam, saying that there was 'no need to delay the talks that could bring an end to this long and bloody war'. He said that the United States was prepared to move rapidly towards negotiations, going as far as naming the veteran American diplomat W. Averell Harriman (1891-1986) as the US representative at such talks. He announced a restriction of bombing to the area south of the twentieth parallel, close to the Demilitarized Zone (DMZ), meaning that Hanoi would no longer be a target and went on to recognise the divisions in America over the war, warning viewers to 'guard against divisiveness and all its ugly consequences'. He ended, however, with the dramatic words: 'I have concluded that I should not permit the presidency to become involved in the partisan divisions that are developing in this political year... Accordingly, I shall not seek, and I will not accept, the nomination of my party for another term as your president.'

What Johnson did not say was equally interesting. He failed to state that he would not resume bombing if the talks failed and he did not say that he would not increase the number of US troops in Vietnam – there were now 550,000. While certain of Johnson's generals remained hopeful that there would be a return to a more aggressive approach to the war, it would now be up to Clifford to try to bring the war to a conclusion.

The North Vietnamese had already decided to talk before Johnson's televised abdication. Hoping to make an impact on the American domestic audience, they invited Walter Cronkite to Hanoi so that they could explain their new attitude to the war. Cronkite declined the invitation, fearful that it might appear that he was only being invited because of his criticism of the war and that to go would be unpatriotic. Instead a veteran CBS reporter, Charles Collingwood (1917-85), went. During an interview with Collingwood on 5 April, North Vietnamese Foreign Minister Nguyen Duy Trinh (1910-85) announced that North Vietnam was, indeed, prepared to come to the negotiating table. Consequently, amidst an atmosphere of hope, both sides met on 10 April in Paris, the American delegation headed by Harriman and the North Vietnamese by diplomat and veteran politician, Xuan Thuy (1912-85). They began by wrangling over procedural issues and who should be involved. Famously, they even argued over the shape of the conference table around which the negotiators would sit. Harriman had a bombing pause up his sleeve as well as an agreed mutual ceiling on numbers of troops, but the plan was to adopt a tough posture to begin with, especially as Tet had, to American minds at least, weakened Hanoi's bargaining position. The North Vietnamese, on the other hand, were not prepared to make any compromises, hoping that delays to a cessation of bombing would agitate America's anti-war movement still further. Their position was firmly that they were unprepared to enter into substantive discussions until the bombing stopped and America ceased operations in South Vietnam. Johnson believed, in fact, that the North Vietnamese would not negotiate at least until his successor was in office. Within weeks, however, the talks had arrived at a stalemate similar to that of the war itself. The US delegation insisted on the withdrawal of all North Vietnamese troops from South Vietnam while the North Vietnamese representatives insisted on Viet Cong representation in the Saigon government. Naturally, neither side was prepared to move.

For five more years these talks would continue and during this time many more would die. Meanwhile, the United States would be riven by one of the greatest crises in its history.

Change of Commander, Change of Tactics

General Westmoreland's tour of duty ended in June 1968 when he was replaced as commander of MACV by General Creighton Abrams (1914-74) who had been working as deputy-commander of MACV to improve the performance of the ARVN. His good work was demonstrated by its improved efficiency during the Tet Offensive. Westmoreland had conducted an attritional war using 'search-and-destroy' tactics. Abrams changed this to 'clear-and-hold'. US forces, broken up into small units, were used, under his command, to train South Vietnamese civilians to defend their villages from the North Vietnamese. He also worked hard to 'Vietnamise' the ARVN. Commanders tended to stand back and let the Americans control their operations which caused undeniable tension, the

Americans characterising the South Vietnamese troops as lazy and only too willing to avoid arduous decisions and work. He put a great deal of effort into training the South Vietnamese and improving their equipment and also increased the size of the army to 800,000.

Pacification became an important element of Abrams' command. Prior to 1968, the MACV and the Saigon government had not given much consideration to rural South Vietnam. But now, with Viet Cong numbers decimated by Tet, it was becoming possible to gain access to those areas. Although it had gained some defectors from the communist side with promises of amnesties, and had arrested some communist cadres, the Civilian Operations and Revolutionary Development Support (CORDS) initiative had been relatively ineffective. There were signs that, under pressure, the government was beginning to deal with the corruption that blighted it and the rampant inflation the country was experiencing, but little was being done by President Thieu and Prime Minister Ky to alleviate the refugee problem and they and their government were as unpopular as ever.

The 1968 Presidential Election

Following President Johnson's withdrawal from consideration for the Democratic nomination for the 1968 presidential election, Robert Kennedy, Johnson's Vice President Hubert Humphrey (1911-78) and South Dakota Senator George McGovern (1922-2012) joined Eugene McCarthy on the ballot papers at the various primaries. However, it has been suggested that, rather than these candidates, Johnson wanted the Republican nominee, Richard Nixon, to win because he felt that Nixon was more likely to continue his policy in Vietnam.

By now, 400 young Americans were dying every week in Vietnam and the horror of the war was being broadcast on a nightly basis on US television news programmes. There was a fear that the election would be turned into a referendum on the war but

Americans had plenty of other pressing issues to concern them. The summers of the previous three years had seen outbreaks of violence in some of the largest cities in the United States, the poor and the underprivileged – mostly African Americans – venting their frustrations on the nation's streets. Therefore, one of the important questions for voters was whether American taxpayers were prepared to pay more of their hard-earned cash for Lyndon Johnson's anti-poverty programmes. The riots were violent, protesters from the ghettos that blighted America's cities engaging in battles with police and National Guardsmen who were predominantly white. Peace demonstrations were less violent, but a general feeling grew amidst the electorate that law and order needed to be an election issue, although that meant, in reality, something being done about the African American rioters and the hippie demonstrators.

Robert Kennedy's decision to enter the race for the Democratic nomination generated a great deal of resentment in the McCarthy camp. They felt that they had taken the risk by challenging the incumbent and now Kennedy would ride on the coat-tails of that courageous stand. He was being merely opportunistic, McCarthy followers complained. For his part, Kennedy did not believe that Johnson's Great Society concept had made any difference to the plight of those living in poverty in America's inner cities, partly because of the huge expenditure on the war in Vietnam from which he believed the United States should extricate itself.

Just a few days after Johnson's broadcast, America suffered another shock when civil rights leader, Dr Martin Luther King, was shot dead in Memphis. Once again America's cities were ripped apart by rioting. Kennedy heard the news of Dr King's assassination as he was about to speak to a crowd in a predominantly African American part of Indianapolis. He announced the news and followed with a passionate plea that the violence stop. Of course, his own brother's assassination made him especially qualified to talk about such incidents and the passions they arouse. 'In this difficult time for the United States,' he said, 'it is perhaps well to ask what kind of a nation we are and what direction we want to move in.' It was an observation that encapsulated the position in which America found itself at the time, both domestically and in its foreign policy. Kennedy was calling for nothing short of a re-evaluation of American national identity and this would become the overriding theme of his campaigning over the summer months. He won four state primaries – Indiana, Nebraska, South Dakota and California – while McCarthy won six – Wisconsin, Pennsylvania, Massachusetts, Oregon, New Jersey and Illinois. Where they campaigned directly against each other, Kennedy won three and McCarthy won one. Humphrey, meanwhile, did not contest the primaries, focusing instead on winning delegates in states that did not have primaries. The California primary was crucial to both candidates but, after securing a victory by 46 to 42 per cent, Kennedy, now gaining real momentum in the contest and looking as if he would secure the nomination, was tragically assassinated in the ballroom of the Ambassador Hotel in Los Angeles by Sirhan Sirhan in protest at the candidate's support for Israel.

It added to the turmoil America had been in for months. Violence still erupted in reaction to King's murder while fighting in Vietnam continued relentlessly to be beamed into American living rooms. In April, student protesters at Columbia City University in New York occupied the administration buildings and closed down the university. They were removed violently by officers of the NYPD who used tear gas to end the occupation. Over 700 were arrested. The following day, students wielding sticks clashed violently with police officers. There was also trouble at Stanford University in California where protesters set fire to the Reserve Officer Training Corps building. A group of activists founded the Youth International Party – members known as Yippies – and announced that they would be nominating a pig named 'Pigasus the Immortal' as a candidate for the presidency.

With Kennedy gone, Hubert Humphrey looked like winning the Democratic nomination. McCarthy had done far better than expected, but at the national convention it was almost certain that Humphrey's wide support within the party would prevail and deliver him the requisite number of delegate votes. The number of convention votes the primaries had won for McCarthy would be dwarfed by the delegate votes in the hands of local and state party committees who were entirely dependent on the president and vice president for their positions and would inevitably side with Humphrey.

Minnesota Senator Hubert Humphrey was a liberal Democrat who had been a loyal supporter of Lyndon Johnson's Great Society programme and it was for that reason that Johnson had named him as his vice presidential running mate in 1964. He had supported civil rights for African Americans and was fervently anti-communist. He had also been a supporter of containment in Indochina. But, like a number of other Democrats, Humphrey was beginning to have doubts about US involvement in Vietnam, worrying that vital resources were being diverted from the domestic budget and from other important international programmes and policies. Johnson had, in fact, stopped him from attending White House policy discussions because he was increasingly unsupportive. However, the problem for Humphrey was that he was inextricably linked in the public consciousness with Johnson's policies at home and his approach to Vietnam. There was also a danger, with his support for civil rights and for the democratic right of anti-war demonstrators to protest, that he would be seen as soft on the other major issue occupying voters' minds – law and order. Humphrey found himself in a tricky situation, and sometimes appeared not to have a clear position on a number of the key issues.

The Democratic National Convention of 1968 was staged from 26 to 29 August at the International Amphitheatre in Chicago. Humphrey was a certainty to be nominated, but delegates who had backed Kennedy, McCarthy and McGovern, united to try to insert in the Democratic Party platform a call for an end to bombing of North Vietnam and for a coalition government for South Vietnam. Humphrey again found himself in a difficult situation as these moves were very close to what he believed himself, but the delegates rejected the challenge to the government's policy. Although 80 per cent of primary voters had voted for anti-war candidates, Humphrey won the Democratic Party nomination on the first ballot. It was events outside the convention hall that grabbed national and international attention, however. The National Mobilization Committee to End the War in Vietnam and the Yippies had decided to stage a youth festival in Chicago at the same time as the convention. Other groups such as Students for a Democratic Society also became involved. Around 10,000 mostly young people arrived in Chicago to join an anti-war protest in Grant Park but Chicago Mayor Richard J Daley (1902-76) had called in thousands of police and National Guardsmen to prevent them from disrupting the proceedings at the convention. When a young man lowered an American flag, police officers moved into the crowd and began beating him. The crowd reacted violently, throwing rocks and pieces of concrete at the officers. Tear gas was fired into many, Mace was also used and the crowd moved out of the park to avoid being caught up in the chaos. In front of the Hilton Hotel the police charged into the crowd under the gaze of network TV news cameras, the crowd chanting 'The whole world is watching'. There were hundreds of injuries and many were arrested.

The 1968 election featured a third candidate – George Wallace (1919-98), the pugnacious Governor of Alabama. A three-time presidential candidate, the segregationist Wallace would earn the title 'the most influential loser' because of his ability to take white votes from both the major parties. General Curtis LeMay (1906-90), Wallace's running mate, scared everyone by talking about using nuclear weapons. When asked what his response to North Vietnam would be, LeMay is famously supposed to have said: '... they've got to draw in their horns and stop their aggression, or we're going to bomb them back into the Stone Age.'

It has been said that on that night of rioting outside the convention, America probably made up its mind to vote for Richard Milhous Nixon (1913-94), the Republican presidential nominee. Nixon had served for eight years as President Eisenhower's vice president and had been narrowly defeated by John Kennedy in 1960. After he had failed to secure the governorship of California in 1962, he gave a speech in which he blamed the media for his defeat. 'You won't have Nixon to kick around any more,' he told journalists, 'because gentlemen, this is my last press conference.' Until the end of 1967, he had withdrawn from active politics but he was nothing if not politically ambitious and announced his candidature for the Republican nomination which he won easily. The Richard Nixon of the late 1960s was a softer version of the fervent red-baiter of the 1950s. It was clear, however, that he was vehemently against the anti-war protests, viewing them as a threat to the preservation of law and order in America. Thus, in his campaign, he projected himself as the law and order candidate. He mounted a television advertising campaign and, correctly gauging the mood of the American people, promised what he called 'peace with honour' in Vietnam. 'The new leadership will end the war and win the peace in the Pacific,' he said, but he declined to release any details of how he was going to achieve this. Figures in the media began to speak of a 'secret plan'. There was no 'secret plan', however, and Nixon was, indeed, an unlikely peace candidate. He had subscribed to the 'domino theory' espoused by Eisenhower, was a staunch defender of past American presidents' decisions to defend South Vietnam and had, in fact, tried to persuade Eisenhower to send troops to help the French in Indochina. He not only supported Johnson's escalation of American involvement in Vietnam but also thought he should have committed even more American troops and air power to the war effort. Nixon viewed North Vietnam's aggression against South Vietnam as part of a global threat to the security of the world posed by the Soviet Union and China.

By late September 1968, Humphrey was falling far behind Nixon in the polls. It was a desperate time for Humphrey who knew that his only chance of clawing back some ground on the Republican challenger was to distance himself from President Johnson with whom, in the public's mind, he was inextricably linked. Consequently, in a campaign speech in Utah, he promised, 'I would stop the bombing as an acceptable risk for peace.' It did the trick, sending his poll ratings up and bringing in more campaign donations. The peace talks were continuing in Paris and Humphrey's statement provided Averell Harriman with some leverage over the North Vietnamese delegation, the Hanoi representatives agreeing to talk with President Thieu's South Vietnamese representatives if the bombing was halted. In a television broadcast on 31 October, Johnson announced a cessation of bombing and talks would begin, he went on, on 6 November, the day following the election. President Thieu announced, however, that he would not countenance direct talks with the North Vietnamese, thus delaying negotiations, much to the embarrassment of the White House and the dismay of Humphrey for whom the prospect of negotiations might have created a favourable surge in the polls. It had been unlikely anyway that the talks would amount to anything substantial while Johnson refused to recognise the Viet Cong and opposed the idea of their involvement in a coalition involving the communists to govern South Vietnam. Neither were the North Vietnamese going to budge, especially as the Americans had thrown so much at them and they were still standing.

Nixon won the presidential election on 5 November, taking 301 electoral votes while Humphrey won 191 and George Wallace 46. It was much closer in terms of popular vote, Nixon gaining 43.4 to Humphrey's 42.7 per cent. In fact, there were some underhand dealings of the kind that would eventually end the Nixon presidency in disgrace. He had been in touch with Thieu to tell him not to allow any diplomatic breakthroughs that would help Humphrey before the election. Johnson was aware of this through illegal wiretaps that he had ordered on Nixon's phones. He informed Humphrey who chose not to make this information public as it had been obtained through illegal activity, even though it would probably have wrecked Nixon's chances of becoming president. Nixon denied the allegations in a phone call to Johnson and some sources say that it is unlikely anyway that Thieu would have listened to Nixon, and that Humphrey was so closely linked to Johnson's policies in the public mind that he could never have won.

7

'Peace with Honour': President Nixon 1969 to 1973

'Madman Theory' and Triangular Diplomacy

Nixon stated that there was no chance of a 'military victory' in Vietnam but he did say later that he had no intention of becoming 'the first president of the United States to lose a war', a sentiment no doubt shared by his predecessor. Consequently, he decided to use scare tactics against North Vietnam. It was a strategy borrowed from Eisenhower. In 1953, during the Korean War, the Chinese and the North Koreans had agreed to talks but were also still engaged in fighting, hoping that they could gain leverage from success on the battlefield to improve their positions at the peace negotiations. Eisenhower let it be known through covert sources that he would not be averse to using atomic weapons if progress was not forthcoming. His brinkmanship worked and the peace negotiations moved forward. The new president believed he could use the same tactic to similar effect. He told White House Chief of Staff, H.R. Haldeman (1926-93):

'I call it the Madman Theory, Bob. I want the North Vietnamese to believe that I've reached the point where I might do anything to stop the war. We'll just slip the word to them that "For God's sake, you know Nixon is obsessed about communists. We can't restrain him when he's angry — and he has his hand on the nuclear button" – and Ho Chi Minh himself will be in Paris in two days begging for peace.'

Haldeman, H. R., *The Ends of Power*,
Times Books, New York, 1978

Another option was for Nixon to persuade the Soviet Union and China to put pressure on the DRV to take the talks more seriously and strive to find a way to end the war. There was little doubt that the Russians were flagging in their support of North Vietnam which was, after all, really outside their sphere of interest. Furthermore, the aid the Russians were pouring into the DRV was sapping the Soviet economy and damaging their relations with the United States. At the same time, however, they could not afford to walk away from North Vietnam because that risked exposing them to charges of neglecting their role in the fight against what they and the Chinese termed 'American imperialism'. The Chinese would have a field day if they did. Nixon was of the opinion, therefore, that the Russians would welcome any opportunity to bring the war to a conclusion. He had bargaining chips too – wheat supplies, access to modern technology and an agreement on nuclear weapons. All of these were of far greater importance to the Soviet Union than a corner of Southeast Asia far from the mother country. The caveat, however, was that the Soviet Union should reduce its activity in other regions where there was tension, such as Berlin and the Middle East. This was a technique that Nixon named 'linkage' and it was supposed to connect military and economic matters, progress in one area being dependent on progress in the other. In the case of the Chinese, they had been isolated for years. As Nixon wrote a year before his election to the presidency, 'There is no place on this small planet for a billion of its potentially most able people to live in angry isolation'. He surmised that Mao Zedong might be open to some kind of rapprochement with the United States, thus providing him with leverage over the Soviet Union. In order to achieve this, Nixon thought, the Chinese might be willing to persuade Ho Chi Minh to work towards a settlement in Vietnam. To orchestrate this foreign policy, Nixon appointed Henry Kissinger (born 1923) as his Secretary of State.

Kissinger had arrived in New York from Nazi Germany in 1938, with his Jewish parents. In the Second World War, he had been drafted into the US infantry and after the war had worked in the military administration that ran Germany. Graduating from Harvard, he worked with the Council on Foreign Affairs, advised New York Mayor and presidential candidate Nelson Rockefeller and ran Operation Pennsylvania for President Johnson, one of several attempts to persuade the North Vietnamese to come to the negotiating table. He was also Harvard professor of international relations. Kissinger used his experience in the Johnson administration to advise Nixon's presidential campaign and Nixon would come to work closely with him, often bypassing other members of his Cabinet, Congress or the American public in order to achieve his aim of extracting the United States quickly and successfully from the war. The two shared a love of secrecy and intrigue and while Nixon sought the most effective person to help him implement his policies, the well-connected Kissinger sought access to the power that he craved.

The Secret Bombing of Cambodia

The notion of a 'secret plan' still hung around the Nixon White House but in reality Nixon had no concrete idea what he was going to do except bring an end to the war as fast as he could. He had no intention of his presidency becoming mired in the Vietnam War in the same way as Johnson's had and had long been a supporter of the greater use of American air power in Vietnam. He had argued against bombing halts as he believed the bombing was the only thing

America could bring to the negotiating table in Paris. Operation Rolling Thunder, which had lasted from 1965 until Johnson stopped it at the end of October 1968, had done a great deal of damage to the infrastructure of North Vietnam. More than half of the country's bridges had been destroyed and petrol storage facilities and power plants had been decimated. The CIA estimated in January 1968 that around 1,000 North Vietnamese – most of them civilians – were being killed every week by the bombs. The bombing campaign suffered from the same flaws as the rest of the war, however, its success being measured by the number of sorties flown and the number of bombs dropped. Of course, what really should have mattered was how effective these sorties were in terms of achieving their objectives. To bolster the number of sorties sometimes eight planes would be dispatched with small bomb loads when in actual fact the loads could have been delivered by just two planes.

Diplomatic resolution to the war was still not forthcoming, forcing Nixon to turn to conventional military options. Like Johnson, he came to believe that, in order to persuade the North Vietnamese that America's commitment to South Vietnam was genuine, he was going to have to escalate US involvement. Of course, he knew full well that this strategy had not worked for Johnson, that the Vietnamese just kept supplying fresh troops to replace those that the Americans had killed. Following consultation with his advisers, he concluded that one of the problems was the neutrality of Laos and Cambodia. The Americans were prohibited by their neutrality from fighting in these countries, but the North Vietnamese and Viet Cong were still establishing bases and supply routes around the borders of Laos and Cambodia, safe from American attacks. Nixon and Kissinger decided, therefore, to expand the war with the secret bombardment of Cambodia, including the use of B-52 bombers. Sometimes these attacks were followed up with strikes across the border by US Special Forces but everything was hushed up in order to forestall the inevitable political backlash back home. Wiretaps were put on the phones of members of the National Security Council following the publication of an article about the attacks on Cambodia in the *New York Times*. Such illegal and covert activity became the leitmotif of the Nixon presidency and would lead, ultimately, to Watergate and his resignation. His administration also entered into secret diplomacy with the North Vietnamese, proffering a proposal that the United States and the DRV should withdraw forces from South Vietnam and negotiations should begin between Thieu's government and the NLF with the aim of achieving 'political reconciliation'. Meanwhile, Nixon instructed Kissinger to inform the Soviets that an improvement in relations between them and the United States would only be possible after the end of the war in Vietnam. With this he hoped to force the Russians to put pressure on Hanoi. It was another example of 'linkage'.

'Vietnamisation'

The fighting continued and the North Vietnamese continued to move men and supplies along the Ho Chi Minh Trail and into South Vietnam. Troops of the ARVN had played only a small part in the fighting since 1965. They were largely infantry troops and were more suited to local security operations than to fighting against large North Vietnamese combat units best dealt with by the more powerful and better equipped American tactical units. But General Westmoreland had increased their involvement in 1967 and, when peace negotiations began and it looked more likely that the Americans and North Vietnamese would withdraw their troops at some point, their participation was increased still further. Nonetheless, American troops still did the lion's share of the fighting. As soon as Nixon took office, he resolved that the United States should provide arms and logistical support to the Allied forces that were engaged in the fighting, but no US combat troops – especially ground troops – should be involved. In April 1969, the new Secretary of Defense, Melvin Laird (born 1922), commissioned a withdrawal plan from American military chiefs and in June, at a conference on Midway Island, Nixon informed President Thieu that 25,000 troops were going to be withdrawn from Vietnam immediately. In September it was announced that a further 35,000 were being withdrawn and December saw an announcement of the withdrawal of another 50,000. The plan was for a gradual but total withdrawal, leaving an improved ARVN to take care of security and a government that was capable of managing the war and the country without external support. It was hoped this would be beneficial to the Nixon administration in terms of public opinion and that it would create confidence in the Saigon government which could perhaps even encourage the North Vietnamese to take the negotiations more seriously. There was no comprehensive plan. Rather, it seemed to depend on American public opinion, how much improvement the ARVN displayed and what Viet Cong activity was like at the time. The course was set, however, and there was no denying that involvement of US ground troops in Vietnam was being brought to an end.

'Vietnamisation' was the name the Nixon administration gave to his policy which aimed 'to expand, equip and train South Vietnam's forces and assign them to an ever-increasing combat role, at the same time steadily reducing the number of US combat troops' as the newly appointed Secretary of Defense put it. Melvin Laird was appointed on 21 January 1969. A senior Republican who had been a Congressman since 1953, Laird had been critical of the Johnson administration's handling of the war, especially its deception about its cost.

For Nixon, Vietnamisation consisted of strengthening and improving the South Vietnamese armed forces as well as extending the pacification programme. In the first of these elements, it would be necessary to use US helicopter support, but that would involve US personnel. It was decided, therefore, to train ARVN troops to fly them. Unfortunately, this was a process that would take two years – most of the candidates had to be taught English before they could learn to fly.

Of course, withdrawing troops did not exactly enhance the American negotiating position in Paris and there seemed to be no plans to help the Thieu government to make itself efficient, effective and, above all, free of corruption. Furthermore, there was no evidence that the Saigon administration and the ARVN were actually capable of becoming what the United States wanted. To both North Vietnamese and South Vietnamese, Vietnamisation was nothing more than an effort by the US government to come up with a way to withdraw from Vietnam, leaving a government and army that were capable of lasting for as long as they could. As North Vietnamese Colonel Quach Hai Luong said: 'If before we had to fight two forces – both Saigon and US forces – then with Vietnamisation we only had to deal with one and a half. And the result was that the Saigon forces could not endure.' (Prados, John, *The Hidden History of the Vietnam War*, Chicago, Ivan R Dee, 1995).

The ground war continued, but as in the Paris talks, stalemate prevailed. Operation Apache Snow was initiated in May 1969, with the aim of maintaining pressure on communist units and bases in the A Shau Valley, located west of the city of Hue, and bringing a halt to North Vietnamese attacks on the coastal provinces of South Vietnam. Three airborne infantry battalions of the 101st Airborne Division were assigned to the operation – the 3rd Battalion, 187th Infantry Regiment; 2nd Battalion, 501st Parachute Infantry Regiment; and the 1st Battalion, 506th Parachute Infantry Regiment. Two battalions of the ARVN's 1st Division had also been temporarily assigned to the 3rd Brigade. Other major units participating in Apache Snow included the 9th Marine Regiment, 3rd Squadron, 5th Cavalry Regiment and the 3rd ARVN Regiment. On 10 May, American and ARVN forces entered the area, at first encountering only light resistance. The main force of North Vietnamese troops was located, however, in the A Shau Valley, at Ap Bia Mountain which was known to the Americans as Hill 937. The Americans, often unable to pronounce the Vietnamese names of hills, named them after the numbers marked on the contour lines on their maps. So, the top contour line circle on Ap Bia was 937, indicating that it was 937 metres above sea level. Consequently, it was called Hill 937. However, it would become infamous amongst US soldiers as 'Hamburger Hill' because those trying to capture its rugged terrain were 'chewed up like a hamburger'.

The task of capturing the hill was allotted to the 3rd Battalion of the US 187th Infantry and it took them from 11 to 20 May to secure it, fighting on rugged, uninviting terrain covered in triple-canopy jungle with thick bamboo and elephant grass that came up to the waist. Many casualties were incurred – 50 US and ARVN troops losing their lives and more than 400 wounded. It is estimated that at least 630 NVA soldiers died while the number of their wounded is unknown. The losses on Hamburger Hill were not as dramatic as in some previous confrontations in the war, but the battle made a huge impact on public opinion in the United States. Most galling was the fact that, immediately after capturing the hill, the US and ARVN forces simply abandoned it. In fact, the PAVN returned shortly afterwards and reoccupied the hill unchallenged. The Vietnam War, we must remember, was a war fought not to gain territory; it was purely about body count. Americans at home were astonished and horrified that so many young US soldiers had sacrificed their lives for no apparent gain. This feeling of horrified disbelief was exacerbated by the certain knowledge that, before too long, American soldiers would once again be fighting to take Hill 937. It was a gift to the peace movement and a nightmare for the government's PR machine.

Hamburger Hill resulted in a reappraisal of American strategy in Vietnam. Nixon ordered General Abrams to conduct the war 'with a minimum of American casualties', forcing Abrams to bring a halt to his policy of exerting 'maximum pressure' on North Vietnamese forces. Instead, he introduced a strategy of 'protective reaction'. Nixon told him to proceed at all speed with Vietnamisation and also outlined a new policy during a press conference in Guam after meeting President Thieu on Midway Island and announcing the first troop withdrawal. The new policy would become known as the 'Nixon Doctrine' which was formalised in a televised speech to the American people on 3 November 1969:

> 'First, the United States will keep all of its treaty commitments. Second, we shall provide a shield if a nuclear power threatens the freedom of a nation allied with us or of a nation whose survival we consider vital to our security. Third, in cases involving other types of aggression, we shall furnish military and economic assistance when requested in accordance with our treaty commitments. But we shall look to the nation directly threatened to assume the primary responsibility of providing the manpower for its defense.'

Nixon hoped that people would see Vietnamisation, troop withdrawals and a reduction of risk to US soldiers as a sign that he was delivering on his election promise to de-Americanise the war. He also hoped that a reduction in the death toll would take some of the sting out of the peace movement. At the same time, he hoped that more hawkish elements would be pleased that the United States remained committed to South Vietnam. Meanwhile, he persevered with his 'Madman Theory', letting it be known in a document leaked to the press in July that an all-out US naval and air assault on North Vietnam was being planned and that it would involve nuclear weapons. He sent a message to Ho Chi Minh, warning that if no significant progress had been made in Paris by 1 November, the United States would have no option but to use what he described as 'measures of great consequence and great force'. Plans were laid for an operation codenamed 'Duck Hook' or 'Pruning Knife', as it was known by the military. It involved the possible dropping of nuclear bombs on important targets in and around Hanoi, the mining of North Vietnamese ports and air strikes against roads, bridges and passes, including those on the border with China. There would also be attacks using ground troops on other targets across Vietnam. In a memo Kissinger asked Nixon whether they should consider using nuclear weapons and he added, 'To achieve its full effect on Hanoi's thinking, the action must be brutal.' The last five words were underlined. Ultimately, Kissinger recommended that they abandon Duck Hook on 17 October 1969 and Nixon rejected it finally on 1 November. There were several reasons. They were unsure if even action as drastic as this would destroy North Vietnamese resolve; public – and political – support in America for the war was rapidly diminishing; and both Defense Secretary Laird and Secretary of State William P Rogers (1913-2001) were firmly against military escalation. The main problem was that Hanoi was still refusing to contemplate any kind of compromise or deal until its two familiar demands were met – withdrawal of US troops and the removal of Thieu's government. Kissinger had been meeting in secret with them since August. In mid-August, Ho Chi Minh replied to Nixon's letter, rejecting any kind of compromise but not even mentioning the ultimatum Nixon had delivered. Nixon was, naturally, furious but was restrained from any precipitate action by Laird and other advisers.

Meanwhile, Nixon played the 'Madman' card with the Soviet Union. In October, his administration hinted to the Kremlin that 'the madman was loose' and had ordered the United States military to full global war readiness alert – the American population was blissfully unaware – and for three days, to emphasise the fact, US bombers armed with nuclear weapons flew close to the Soviet border.

On 2 September 1969, twenty years to the day after he had used the text of the American Declaration of Independence to proclaim the independence of Vietnam, Ho Chi Minh's fascinating life came to an end. Reluctant to make its national day a day of mourning for their lost leader, the authorities in Hanoi declared his death the following day. He had prepared a testament the previous May that predicted that:

'Our compatriots in the North and South shall be reunited under the same roof. We a small nation, will have earned the unique honour of defeating, through a heroic struggle, two big imperialisms – the French and the American – and making a worthy contribution to the national liberation movement.'

Those who survived him, such as Le Duan (1907-1986), Van Dong and Vo Nguyen Giap, promised to continue the fight until 'there is not a single aggressor in the country'.

Nixon speaks to the 'Silent Majority'

The peace movement had been comparatively quiet in 1969, but on 15 October activists staged the Moratorium to End the War in Vietnam, the largest national protest since the start of the conflict. Peaceful protests were staged in hundreds of cities across the country, including a gathering of 100,000 to hear a speech by anti-war Senator George McGovern in Boston. Millions also demonstrated around the world and the three major networks' news broadcasts that evening were almost entirely devoted to coverage of the events. A month later, a second huge Moratorium march was staged in Washington DC, attended by 500,000 protesters. The previous Thursday, the March Against Death was held in which 40,000 people marched in single file along Pennsylvania Avenue to the White House. The silent parade continued through the night and all of the day following, each marcher carrying a placard bearing the name of a dead American soldier or the name of a Vietnamese village that had been destroyed. In front of the Capitol building, the placards were deposited in coffins. With the demonstrators outside the White House being led by Pete Seeger in singing John Lennon's peace hymn *Give Peace a Chance*, Nixon remained unmoved, saying: '...I understand that there has been, and continues to be, opposition to the war in Vietnam on the campuses and also in the nation. As far as this kind of activity is concerned, we expect it; however under no circumstances will I be affected whatsoever by it.'

His 3 November broadcast in which he proclaimed the Nixon Doctrine was undoubtedly a response to the first Moratorium but is also famous for another phrase – the 'Silent Majority'. In fact, the speech became known as the 'Silent Majority speech'. He pleaded with the nation: 'And so tonight – to you, the great silent majority of my fellow Americans – I ask for your support.' The next day, in a follow-up to the speech, he announced the withdrawal of a further 60,000 troops and cancelled the draft for the rest of 1969. In December, he announced, a Selective Service lottery system would begin. This would dramatically reduce the number of young men being drafted. In the speech, Nixon explained that the United States was faced with two choices regarding Vietnam. The first was 'immediate, precipitate withdrawal'. He did not elaborate on this choice, simply rejecting it out of hand. The second choice was what he termed 'the right way'. This involved, he explained, persevering with the Paris negotiations but if those failed to deliver an honourable American exit from Vietnam, then the programme of Vietnamisation would, allowing forces to be withdrawn according to a schedule and tying in with ARVN's capability to defend their own freedom for themselves.

The United States Invades Cambodia

Little progress was made either on the battlefield or at the negotiation table during the last few months of 1969. Nixon's troop withdrawals were welcomed, but there were still 475,200 US military personnel in Vietnam as the year drew to a close. 11,780 had died during 1969, although this was down on the 16,899 of the previous year which was by far the bloodiest of the war. Work was progressing on Vietnamisation, however, and the ARVN would be built up to a strength of a million men by 1970. They were also being better equipped, armed with the same M-16 automatic rifles and other weapons used by the Americans. The Civilian Operations and Revolutionary Development Support (CORDS) programme pushed Vietnamisation, providing greater security for villagers, seeking out Viet Cong and implementing land reform. General Abrams abandoned his predecessor's big unit strategy and instead worked with the ARVN and CORDS to provide greater security for the South Vietnamese people. Corruption was still rife, desertion from the South Vietnamese army was commonplace and the lack of education of many of the officers and men made it impossible to train them in the use of some of the complex weaponry that was now available to them. American soldiers were suspicious of the will of the South Vietnamese to fight and there was suspicion in return from ARVN troops who saw the erosion in America of the desire to remain involved in Vietnam. There were problems within the US forces, too. With the United States eager to exit from this unwanted war, for many troops it became a matter of just surviving their tour of duty rather than accomplishing the objectives they were being set. There were disciplinary issues and the use of drugs increased.

In March 1970, proclaiming the success of Vietnamisation, Nixon announced that a further 150,000 troops would be withdrawn in the coming year. His secret bombing of Cambodia, Operation Menu, had been intended to destroy the North Vietnamese/NLF headquarters in Cambodia – known to the Americans as the Central Office for South Vietnam, or COSVN. Nixon hoped to show Hanoi that he would take steps that the Johnson administration had refused to countenance, thus forcing them to negotiate seriously in Paris on his terms. But Abrams and the JCS concurred in the view that the bombing of COSVN had failed to destroy it. The North Vietnamese had simply moved their base deeper into Cambodia.

Meanwhile, Cambodia was itself in turmoil. Its head of state for life, Prince Sihanouk (1922-2012), had pursued a policy of neutrality regarding Vietnam but the country was descending into anarchy as rival factions vied for power. The USA backed the Cambodian prime minister, Lon Nol (1913-85), and Sihanouk was deposed. Despite the certain knowledge that an extension of the war would not play well back home, Nixon seized on the moment to authorise the use of American ground troops in Cambodia, sent in to seek out and eliminate COSVN and any NVA troops and Viet Cong that were found. On 30 April 1970, he appeared on television to tell the American people that he had authorised US and South Vietnamese troops to go into Cambodia in response to a plea for help from the Cambodians. 'This is not an invasion of Cambodia,' he said. 'We take this action not for the purpose of expanding the war into Cambodia but for the purpose of ending the war in Vietnam and winning the just peace we all desire.' The end of his speech was more defiant:

'If, when the chips are down, the world's most powerful nation, the United States of America, acts like a pitiful, helpless giant, the forces of totalitarianism and anarchy will threaten free nations and free institutions throughout the world... I would rather be a one-term president and do what I believe is right than to be a two-term president at the cost of seeing America become a second-rate power and to see this nation accept the first defeat in its proud 190-year history.'

The American people were shocked by this new action and began to believe that this was a president who said one thing and did another. The term 'credibility gap' had already been used of

Lyndon Johnson's administration and it would haunt the remainder of President Nixon's time in office as the American media and the American people began to scrutinise his actions ever more closely.

The day after Nixon spoke to the nation, US and ARVN forces crossed the Vietnam-Cambodia border and launched attacks. Twelve ARVN battalions consisting of just fewer than 9,000 troops crossed into the Parrot's Beak region, so named because of its similarity in shape to the bird's beak. There were confrontations but the North Vietnamese, having prior knowledge of the approach of the South Vietnamese, managed to escape west, deeper into Cambodia. The mission evolved, therefore, into a search and destroy operation, US troops leaving the area and ARVN troops seeking out and destroying enemy supply dumps. After three days, the ARVN claimed that it had killed 1,010 North Vietnamese troops and taken prisoner 204. They, in turn, had lost 66 dead and 330 had been wounded. On 1 May, 774 tons of bombs were dropped along the southern edge of an area known as Fishhook before 10,000 US and 5,000 ARVN troops entered Cambodia's Kampong Cham Province to attack the communist stronghold there. Again, however, PAVN forces had wind of the attacks and had moved westwards in the previous days. Although there were skirmishes with the enemy and only 8 Americans had died by 3 May, later in the month there was heavier fighting with significant American casualties. The North Vietnamese always knew of the impending attacks but one person who was left blissfully unaware was new Cambodian leader Lon Nol who found out via a telephone conversation with the head of the US mission.

Huge quantities of supplies and weapons were seized by the US and ARVN forces during these operations. They also succeeded in disrupting the supply route of the North Vietnamese. In total, 383 US soldiers lost their lives and 693 South Vietnamese; 5,534 were wounded of whom 1,525 were Americans; around 11,000 North Vietnamese were killed and 2,500 taken prisoner. It could confidently be said that the military aspect of the Cambodian operation was a great success. Unfortunately for President Nixon, however, it was a public relations disaster and even damaged what support there was for the war in Congress. In fact, Congress took the dramatic step of repealing the 1964 Gulf of Tonkin Resolution that had given the president what amounted to a 'blank cheque' regarding the war in Vietnam. Restrictions were also placed on funds for military operations in Cambodia after 30 June 1970 and an amendment stated that American troops must be withdrawn from Vietnam by 1971.

At the end of 1970, American forces in Vietnam had been reduced by 200,000. There were now 334,600 US military personnel there and during 1970, 6,173 had died, a good deal fewer than the previous year. Nixon had ridden to power on a promise to 'end the war and win the peace' but in 1970 his actions appeared to be delivering just the opposite. The war had spread over the border into Cambodia while at home the violence had reached unprecedented levels. It was becoming obvious that, despite statements to the contrary that espoused a hard line towards Hanoi, the only way Nixon was going to get America out of this situation was with compromise and concession.

The president was very troubled by his unpopularity and worried that Vietnam was going to damage his chances of a second term. There was also a growing unease amongst his fellow conservatives in Congress. They had been the basis of his support on Capitol Hill but now they worried that the war was threatening their seats in the congressional elections taking place that November. '...when the right starts wanting to get out,' Nixon told Kissinger, 'that's our problem.' The problem was a big one and one that had to be solved before the 1972 presidential election if Nixon and Kissinger were to survive and if the United States was not to suffer huge embarrassment.

The Kent State University Killings

Naturally, the incursion into Cambodia evoked outrage in the United States and there were protests on the streets and on the campuses of the country's universities. It was presented by the media and several prominent Americans as an irresponsible act. Many found it hard to believe that Nixon would even contemplate such an action when the United States was supposed to be winding down its involvement in Vietnam. The protests spread across the country, but one, above all, came to gain a position of notoriety in American public consciousness.

Demonstrations against the invasion had begun at Kent State University in Ohio on 1 May 1970 when 500 students protested on a grassy knoll in the centre of the campus. Trouble broke out in the town of Kent at midnight when people began throwing beer bottles at police officers and smashing shop windows. After officers from outside the town were brought in to bolster the local force, Kent Mayor LeRoy Satrom (1919-2004) declared a state of emergency and the crowds were forced by tear gas back towards the university campus. The following day, the National Guard was called in as a major demonstration continued on campus and protesters set fire to the university's Reserve Officer Training Corps building. As they tried to extinguish the blaze, several firefighters and police officers were struck by missiles thrown by the large crowd that had gathered. Next day, an emotional Ohio Governor James Rhodes (1909-2001) pounded his fists on the desk in front of him and angrily denounced the protesters as '...worse than the Brownshirts, and the communist element, and also the Night Riders, and the vigilantes. They're the worst type of people that we harbour in America.' The National Guard declared a curfew that night and forced the students back into their dorms.

On Monday 4 May university authorities tried to ban a protest planned for midday. Nonetheless, around 2,000 people arrived on the university's Commons ready to demonstrate. As the first speaker launched into his speech, National Guard troopers tried to break up the rally, action that was claimed by some to be illegal but which the United States Court of Appeals for the Sixth Circuit later ruled was, in fact, legal. The students were told that, if they failed to disperse, they faced arrest but the response was a hail of rocks. The Guard retreated and returned with tear gas while the students again threw rocks and chanted, 'Pigs off campus!' The Guard now advanced towards the students with bayonets fixed, the protesters retreating. At one point a group of them kneeled down and took aim with their rifles but they stood up again without firing. The students had now been cleared from the Commons area and were scattered around the campus but although many had left the scene, some remained, throwing missiles at the National Guard. At 12.24 pm, after Sergeant Myron Pryor suddenly opened fire on the students with a .45 pistol, other Guardsmen turned and fired on them. Of the 76 National Guardsmen on duty, 29 fired their weapons, discharging a total of 67 rounds and, as the sound of gunfire died down, four students lay dead. Nine had been wounded. Two of the dead had merely been walking from one class to another; they had played no part in the protests. Pictures of the dead and wounded appeared on television and in newspapers around the world, and anger at the United States' invasion of Cambodia was heightened by the incident. There were protests on campuses across the country and 450 universities closed as students went on strike. At one New York university a banner was hung from a window stating, 'They can't kill us all'. Five days after the shootings, as 100,000 people marched in Washington DC, the president was taken to Camp David for two days for his own protection. Protesters smashed windows, slashed car tyres and caused mayhem in the capital. As White House Counsel, Charles Colson (1931-2012) stated: 'This is not the greatest democracy in the world. This is a nation at war with itself'.

On 13 June, Nixon established the President's Commission on

Campus Unrest – the Scranton Commission. The Commission warned that America was 'so polarized' that there was a grave danger of the campuses once again erupting in violence and even a danger that it would threaten 'the very survival of the nation'. It stated that the rifts in American society were 'as deep as any since the Civil War' and argued that 'nothing is more important than an end to the war in Vietnam'. It found that the shootings at Kent State were unjustified and blamed them on inadequate discipline. Although no criminal charges were brought against them, civil actions by the families of the dead resulted in payments being made to them by the state.

The My Lai Massacre

As if it was not painful enough for the American people to see students being murdered for protesting against the war, they were now faced with what was possibly the most shocking episode of the entire conflict – the massacre at My Lai.

C Company of the 1st Battalion, 20th Infantry Regiment, 11th Brigade of the 23rd Infantry Division had been in Vietnam since December 1967. By the middle of March the following year it had suffered 28 casualties, 5 of whom died, mostly as a result of mines or booby-traps. Following the Tet Offensive, US military intelligence calculated that the 48th Battalion of the NLF was dispersed around the village of Son My in Quang Ngai Province, a region in the South Central Coast area of South Vietnam. My Lai was a settlement within that network of hamlets. C Company was tasked with finding and destroying the remnants of the 48th Battalion, Brigade Commander Colonel Oran K. Henderson (1920-98) leaving his subordinates in no doubt about their mission. He told them 'to go in there aggressively, close with the enemy and wipe them out for good.'

As they prepared to attack, the men of the unit were told by their commanding officer, Captain Ernest Medina (born 1936), that as all civilian residents in the area would have set out for the market by seven in the morning, anyone that was left would inevitably be a member of the National Liberation Front or NLF sympathisers and was to be killed. He is reported to have said: 'They're all VC, now go and get them'. At 7.30 on the morning of 16 March 1968, the 100 men of C Company jumped out of helicopters at Son Mai after the ground had been prepared with a short artillery and helicopter gunship barrage. They were not fired on as they landed, but they still suspected that there were Viet Cong in the area, probably hiding in the huts or in underground shelters. The villagers, many of whom were still preparing for the market, were herded into an open area and the killing began. One soldier bayonetted a villager without warning and then shoved another villager into a well and threw a grenade after him. Around 20 women and children who fell to their knees near a temple were killed with a shot to the head. About 80 villagers were rounded up and walked to an irrigation ditch on the eastern edge of the settlement. Lieutenant William Calley (born 1943), leading the 1st Platoon, gave orders for all to be shot and joined in, this despite the desperate pleas of the villagers as they tried to protect their screaming children that they were not Viet Cong. Private First Class Paul Meadlo later claimed that even when he was shooting mothers with babies in their arms, he was convinced that they were booby-trapped with grenades. Another later testified how:

> 'A lot of women had thrown themselves on top of the children to protect them, and the children were alive at first. Then, the children who were old enough to walk got up and Calley began to shoot the children.'

One helicopter pilot tried to stop the killing. Warrant Officer Hugh Thompson Jr. (1943-2006) landed his craft with the intention of flying a number of villagers out, telling his crew that if the C Company soldiers started shooting while he got the villagers out of the ditch they had been forced into, they should open fire on the soldiers. Thompson reported the incident to his commanding officer. Initially, it was officially reported as a 'fierce fire fight' during which 128 Viet Cong and 22 civilians were killed and General Westmoreland congratulated the unit. The cover-up continued with a report that stated that 20 civilians had been inadvertently killed at My Lai but the story was finally broken on the Associated Wire Service on 12 November by investigative journalist Seymour Hersh (born 1937) after interviews with Lieutenant Calley. Private Meadlo was interviewed on CBS News and pictures of the massacred villagers appeared in the Cleveland newspaper the *Plain Dealer*.

A review of the incident ordered by the Secretary of the Army and the Army Chief of Staff was highly critical but sought to put the blame on four officers who by this time were dead. Eventually, however, Lieutenant Calley was charged with a number of counts of premeditated murder while 25 other officers and men were charged with related crimes. Calley maintained throughout his trial that he was merely following the orders of Captain Medina but, found guilty of the murder of not less than 20 people, he was sentenced to life imprisonment. Two days after the guilty verdict, however, amid great controversy, President Nixon intervened and had Calley released from armed custody and placed under house arrest pending his appeal. Although the conviction was upheld by the Army Court of Military Review in 1973 and the US Court of Military Appeals in 1974, his sentence was reduced to 20 years. In fact, he served only three and a half years under house arrest before being paroled.

Calley's was the only conviction for the massacre. Forty years later, in 2009, he finally made a public apology for My Lai, saying: 'There is not a day that goes by that I do not feel remorse for what happened that day in My Lai.'

Looking for the Exit

The secret Paris negotiations that had been ongoing since 21 February 1970 were interrupted by the Cambodian incursion but Kissinger, who had met with North Vietnamese representative Le Duc Tho (1911-90) on three occasions before the invasion, resumed clandestine meetings on 7 September. Even Secretary of State Rogers and Secretary of Defense Laird were unaware of these discussions. President Thieu was also unaware of the talks, Nixon and Kissinger having promised him that there would be no peace settlement without his agreement. This time Kissinger changed tack. He proposed a programme of complete withdrawal of US forces within twelve months but on this occasion it was not linked to a reciprocal withdrawal of North Vietnamese troops from South Vietnam. He also informed Le Duc Tho that the United States was prepared to agree to an election in South Vietnam, in both the areas that the Saigon government controlled as well as in other parts of the country. The chief North Vietnamese negotiator in Paris, Xuan Thuy – described by one American attendee as 'a top-drawer negotiator, a dreadful fellow to face across the table day after day' – continued to maintain the DRV's insistence that there would be no progress while Thieu and Ky were in office in Saigon.

Desperate to find a way out, Nixon and Kissinger introduced an idea that had been knocking about for years, the notion of a 'standstill ceasefire'. It involved both sides agreeing to a ceasefire and staying in the same place while an international conference attempted to reach a settlement acceptable to all parties. Naturally, this was not to the liking of President Thieu who foresaw North Vietnamese troops remaining forever in the areas they had occupied and South Vietnam effectively being partitioned. Nixon acknowledged these dangers and Kissinger was not terribly keen on it but they had nowhere else to go if they were to avoid even worse violence in America than had hitherto been seen. The president announced the plan during a television broadcast on 7 October 1970. He also took the opportunity to remind his audience that he had already brought home 165,000 American troops from Vietnam, adding that he intended to repatriate a further 90,000 by spring 1971. He awoke the following morning to unaccustomed praise from Congress, even from anti-war advocates such as Senators George McGovern and Mark Hatfield (1922-2011) who were amongst those who signed a resolution approving the plan. Even the press supported it. Kissinger had been pessimistic about their chances for success but noted to aides that it was in reality more than Nixon had intimated. Scrapping the requirement for mutual withdrawal of troops was a major concession. The one sticking point, however, was Thieu. The Americans would permit North Vietnamese troops to remain in South Vietnam only if Thieu was allowed to retain his position. Again Hanoi stubbornly declined any compromise that involved Thieu remaining in office. It seems, though, that Nixon was being somewhat economic with the truth in his televised speech and the North Vietnamese were well aware of this. The following day, he conceded to journalists that he had not watered down his policy. His troop withdrawal was still on condition that North Vietnam did the same thing. Nothing had really changed and it would appear to the more cynical mind that Nixon had only proposed the idea in order to placate the American electorate prior to the November elections, something that Kissinger said 'would give us some temporary relief from public pressures'.

The ARVN Invades Laos

Aid and military equipment continued to pour into South Vietnam from America to the extent that, by December 1971, the ARVN could be said to be one of the best equipped armed forces in the world. US planes continued to bomb North Vietnamese supply lines in Cambodia and Laos as well as strategic targets in North Vietnam itself. On 8 February 1971, the ARVN launched Operation Lam Son 719 – named after an ancient Vietnamese victory over the Chinese – with the objective of destroying a major North Vietnamese supply depot that was located at Tchepone in Laos and disrupting the Ho Chi Minh Trail, part of which passed through the southeastern part of the country. It is now estimated that since 1966, the North Vietnamese had used this route to transport 630,000 men, 100,000 tons of food, 400,000 weapons of all kinds and 50,000 tons of ammunition. The communist political movement, the Pathet Lao, was an ally of Hanoi and had long been conducting an insurrection against the government of Laos. The CIA had already covertly trained the indigenous Hmong people in Laos to fight the Pathet Lao and, of course, tens of thousands of bombs had already been dropped on the Ho Chi Minh Trail within the country. Nixon and Kissinger believed there would probably be a large communist push in the lead-up to the next American presidential election, due to take place in November 1972. To make this happen, the North Vietnamese would have to transport large numbers of men and quantities of equipment along the trail and into South Vietnam. The campaign would be a severe test for Nixon's and Abrams' Vietnamisation, signalling how far the ARVN had come in fending for itself. Victory would be a further morale boost for the ARVN, having already gained in confidence during the previous year's incursion into Cambodia. A successful campaign would bolster the view that, should the United States pull out of Vietnam altogether, the ARVN could, conceivably, look after itself. In fact, United States forces were prohibited by law from setting foot on Laotian territory – a congressional amendment passed after the Cambodian incursion prevented the president from ordering American ground troops into Cambodia or Laos. In addition, the catastrophic reaction in the United States to the invasion of Cambodia meant that any use of American soldiers on the ground in Laos was unthinkable. The American military, therefore, merely provided air, logistical and artillery support from across the border. It was the first time the ARVN went into battle without US military advisers and it did not go well. As Henry Kissinger himself put it: '...the operation, conceived in doubt and assailed by skepticism, proceeded in confusion.'

Tchepone, by this time razed to the ground by the American aerial bombardment, was reached by 6 March but there was savage fighting en route, the ARVN force of 21,000 men encountering a similar-sized, but well-equipped, force of PAVN. If the operation had been undertaken at the end of the rainy season, when the North Vietnamese would have been undersupplied, instead of three months later, when they had been re-supplied more than adequately, it might have gone better for the South Vietnamese. It was also suspected that many of the officers of the invading force actually had North Vietnamese sympathies. To make matters worse, they were briefed about the operation only at the last minute and press reports alerted the communists to the impending attack. It all started to go very wrong as the ARVN began to withdraw. A force of 36,000 PAVN counter-attacked and 2,000 ARVN died in the chaos while a large quantity of tanks, artillery and other equipment was abandoned. American planners had actually estimated that it would take a force of around 60,000 troops to achieve the desired results; Thieu had sent only 30,000 and they were inexperienced. Their target was also within easy range of large North Vietnamese and Viet Cong units.

The number of casualties incurred during Lam Son 719 made it impossible for any major offensive to be launched by the PAVN in 1971 and the ARVN now had bought itself more time to prepare for the inevitable American exit. But the Ho Chi Minh Trail remained viable as a conduit for men and weapons and the failings of the South Vietnamese army had been exposed for all to see. It was a complex situation, however. Senior Vietnamese soldiers had enjoyed the tutelage of the Americans for ten years, some of them at bases in the United States. But it was apparent from Lam Son that little of that training had sunk in. Part of the problem lay with the government they were serving. The Thieu regime was paranoid about the possibility of a *coup d'état*, meaning that the last thing it wanted to see were strong generals who might prove a threat. Therefore, they rewarded and promoted those who showed loyalty to them, regardless of competence. There was wealth to be gained from being subservient to the government and, if that meant not taking any risks and accepting defeat, then so be it.

Nixon told the nation on 7 April 1971, that the Laos venture proved that 'Vietnamisation has succeeded' but the rumour mill and the media suggested otherwise. In Saigon, the South Vietnamese, observing the failure of their army and the prospect of life without US support, took to the streets, demonstrating in front of American offices and businesses and setting fire to American vehicles.

Morale amongst US servicemen was also suffering. Boredom and frustration were making the drug problem increasingly serious and it was estimated that around 65,000 US troops were using drugs. They were cheap, and heroin, opium, amphetamines and LSD were readily available. The authorities introduced urine analysis tests that could be administered at any time, sometimes several times a day. There was also the murderous practice of 'fragging'. In cases where a commander of a unit was incompetent or was ordering his men to take unnecessary risks, soldiers sometimes took matters into their own hands, killing the officer in question with a fragmentation grenade. The beauty of it was that nothing could be traced back to the perpetrator as the grenade was destroyed in the blast. There were an estimated 200 instances of fragging during the Vietnam War. Another symptom of the malaise that was hanging over US soldiers was the splitting of units into factions – black, New York liberals, segregationists from the south and so on. Racial tensions sometimes ran high. Soldiers often slept with their guns at their sides, prepared for an attack by a colleague in the night. The issue was really the perceived futility of the war. Everyone was merely waiting for the politicians to devise a way out for America that would not be demeaning or damaging to the United States' standing in the world. In polls conducted around this time, public confidence in Nixon's presidency fell to 50 per cent, the lowest since he had taken office; support for his conduct of the war was even worse, slumping to just 34 per cent; and faced with the statement that America's involvement in the war in Vietnam was morally wrong, 51 per cent of those questioned agreed.

In late April, the demos started again, now with the added, very poignant participation of members of the organisation Vietnam Veterans Against the War (VVAW). 200,000 marched to a rally in Washington where VVAW staged a protest from 19 to 23 April called Operation Dewey Canyon III, named after two brief invasions of Laos by US and ARVN forces and described by the veterans as 'a limited incursion into the country of Congress'. As part of the demonstration, a group of more than 50 veterans marched to the Pentagon where they tried to surrender themselves as war criminals. Later that week, 800 veterans threw their medals onto the steps of the Capitol. That same week, the future Secretary of State in the Obama administration, John Kerry (born 1943), represented VVAW before the Fulbright Committee. Kerry, who had won three Purple Hearts in Vietnam, told the committee: 'Someone has to die so that President Nixon won't be, and these are his words, "the first President to lose a war".' He continued, 'How do you ask a man to be the last man to die in Vietnam? How do you ask a man to be the last man to die for a mistake?' His concluding remarks to the committee were, indeed, powerful:

'Our determination [is] to undertake one last mission, to reach out and destroy the last vestige of this barbaric war... and... 30 years from now... we will be able to say "Vietnam" and... mean... the place where America finally turned and where soldiers like us helped in the turning.'

The 'Pentagon Papers'

On 13 June 1971, President Nixon and Secretary of State Kissinger were outraged by the publication of a series of lengthy articles in the *New York Times*. Dubbed the 'Pentagon Papers' by the media, the articles were based on a huge collection of secret government memoranda on the war that had been put together and analyzed by the Defense Department during the Johnson presidency. It represented a history of United States' political and military involvement in Vietnam, between 1945 and 1967. The documents were leaked to the press by Daniel Ellsberg (born 1931) who worked for the think tank RAND Corp. A former marine, Ellsberg had been supportive of American involvement in Vietnam but had become critical of the conduct of the war, believing that many of the decisions that had led to the escalation of the conflict had been made erroneously, more often to suit the needs of US politicians than to actually find a political and military solution to the problem in Southeast Asia.

Robert McNamara had started it when he created the Vietnam Study Task Force in June 1967 to write a history of the Vietnam War that would be of help to future generations in policy making. However, he failed to inform either President Johnson or Secretary of State Dean Rusk about the project. McNamara denied that he actually intended to give the documents to his friend Robert Kennedy to help him in his bid for the presidency. The study, consisting of 3,000 pages of historical analysis and 4,000 pages of government documents and classified 'Top Secret – Sensitive', was delivered to McNamara's successor Clark Clifford in January 1969, shortly before Richard Nixon's inauguration. Fifteen copies were produced, and RAND Corp where Ellsberg worked was given two copies. Clifford claims he never read it.

The 'Pentagon Papers' revealed that the government had realised early in the war that it could not be won and that, if the US continued to fight in Vietnam, there would be considerably more casualties than was ever admitted to the American public. An editor at the *New York Times* later wrote that the 'Pentagon Papers' '...demonstrated, among other things, that the Johnson Administration had systematically lied, not only to the public but also to Congress, about a subject of transcendent national interest and significance'. Amongst other things, the documents acknowledged the key role played by the US government in the coup in which Ngo Dinh Diem was deposed and assassinated and stated that the United States planned operations specifically to provoke the North Vietnamese into making a major military assault. Even though the 'Pentagon Papers' dealt primarily with the Johnson administration, Nixon immediately realised the damage that could be done to his 1972 re-election campaign and tried to stop publication, but the Supreme Court denied his appeal. The president was already incandescent with rage about the criticism of his actions and had asked the Justice Department to take out injunctions against the Vietnam Veterans' Dewey Canyon III protest, while his staff made attacks on the credibility of John Kerry. The White House also began to harass Daniel Ellsberg, described rather extravagantly by Henry Kissinger as 'the most dangerous man in America today'. Kissinger was, of course, worried that his diplomatic efforts would founder as a result of the leaking of the 'Pentagon Papers'. He was personally involved as he had consulted Ellsberg on Vietnam in the transition period between the Johnson and Nixon administrations. Having once sung his praises, he now described Ellsberg to Nixon as a 'fanatic' and even a 'drug abuser'. As part of his fightback, Nixon ordered an investigation of Ellsberg. White House official Egil 'Bud' Krogh (born 1939) and a White House lawyer, David Young (born 1936), were appointed to head up a 'Special Investigations Unit' at the White House that was to investigate leaks by staff in the administration. As they were plugging leaks, Young came up with the name 'Plumbers' for them. It would stick and the 'Plumbers' would become notorious during the Watergate scandal. Nixon's

Special Counsel, Charles Colson, brought in experts in the dark arts of spying, espionage and surveillance – men such as former CIA operative E. Howard Hunt (1918-2007) and retired FBI agent G. Gordon Liddy (born 1930). Amongst the tasks they took on was the compilation of a list of 200 enemies of the president that included actors Gregory Peck and Carol Channing, American football player Joe Namath and a number of journalists. As part of the ongoing campaign against Daniel Ellsberg, Hunt and his team of 'Plumbers' were ordered to break into the office of Ellsberg's psychiatrist, Lewis Fielding. Of course, their later break-in on 17 June 1972 at the Democratic National Committee headquarters at the Watergate office complex in Washington DC would result in jail-time for the 'Plumbers' and a number of White House officials. It would also bring an end to Richard Nixon's presidency.

Compromise and Concession

By mid-1971, President Nixon was depressed. He had failed to convince the public, the media, Congress or the judiciary that the 'Pentagon Papers' were profoundly damaging to the United States and should be suppressed. He was often overwhelmed by self-pity, a victim of the growing anti-war feeling of the media and the American public. It sometimes entered his head that the best thing would be to blow North Vietnam off the face of the earth and he often ranted to Kissinger about the possibility of doing just that. Then he would relent and accept that negotiating was the only way out. Kissinger returned to the negotiating table in Paris in late May, the talks continuing inconclusively into 1972, the sticking point, as ever, the status of the Saigon regime following a troop withdrawal. Kissinger, for his part, worried that any concessions would lead to further demands and the United States being held to ransom. He was also concerned about how Thieu would react. He was aware of the chaos that ensued after Diem was deposed and feared a chaotic finale to the war that would leave America, Nixon and himself severely damaged. The global perception of the United States was at stake and a shameful end to the war would, he said, 'leave deep scars on our society, fueling impulses for recrimination'.

Another proposal came from Kissinger's side. On 31 May, he offered to withdraw American forces six months after a ceasefire agreement was signed. It did not even demand the withdrawal of North Vietnamese troops but stipulated that Hanoi would stop sending men along the Ho Chi Minh Trail into the south and that American prisoners of war would be released. It was leaving the political issues of Vietnam to be dealt with by the people of Vietnam and represented significant progress. It would, in fact, form the basis of the agreement that was eventually reached in 1973. The response from Le Duc Tho was an agreement to the ceasefire idea and the release of POWs but he added that the United States should stop its bombing of North Vietnam and should pay reparations. What was different about this proposal was that it did not contain the familiar demand for Thieu and the Saigon regime to be removed before the North Vietnamese would contemplate a cease-fire. Why, at this point, were both sides making such significant concessions? For Nixon, it was obvious that Vietnamisation had failed and he was also under considerable pressure in view of the forthcoming American presidential election. Hanoi had its own problems, however. The fighting in Laos had been extremely costly, in terms of casualties, and the North Vietnamese were also being pressured by their allies, the Soviet Union and China, to adopt a more flexible attitude to negotiations. Still, however, neither side accepted the other's proposal and, while they continued to negotiate in Paris, the fighting continued.

It was later claimed by the communists that during this time, Kissinger missed an opportunity to bring the war to a satisfactory conclusion. An election was scheduled in South Vietnam for 3 October 1971 and Vice President Ky and ARVN General Duong Van

'Big' Minh (1916-2001) were considering running against Thieu. Le Duc Tho proposed to Kissinger that, if the United States withdrew its support from Thieu, the election would probably be won by a candidate who would be in favour of working out an accommodation with the Viet Cong. If Thieu were to lose the election legally, the stumbling block in the talks would have been eliminated and the United States could happily say that it had happened democratically. Thus, the North Vietnamese would work with the Americans towards a peace agreement. Nixon and Kissinger, however, maintained their unrelenting support of President Thieu and, after Ky was disqualified from standing in the election by Thieu, Minh realised he had no chance of victory and withdrew. Thieu was elected to serve another term as President of South Vietnam. Of course, there was no guarantee that Ky or Minh – in the unlikely event of either of them winning – would have welcomed the Viet Cong in Saigon, especially as America was a much more lucrative option for them and for South Vietnam.

By 1972, despite everything, there were some facts that supported President Nixon's claim to be reducing the role of the United States in Vietnam. There were 400,000 fewer American troops, for instance, than when he had taken office. Numbers of American casualties were also drastically down, to the extent that there were now fewer than 10 a week. Nixon tried to demonstrate his good intentions by revealing to the American public that Kissinger had been engaged in secret talks with Hanoi, but, of course, as the American presence in South Vietnam diminished, Kissinger was losing his bargaining chips at the negotiating table. This would also inevitably lead to cuts in aid to South Vietnam, since Senators would no longer feel obliged to agree to increased budgets to support American soldiers risking their lives on the battlefield.

'Ping-Pong Diplomacy'

On 20 August 1968, forces of the Soviet Union and its Warsaw Pact allies had shocked the world by invading Czechoslovakia to bring an end to the reforms being initiated by the government of Alexander Dubcek (1921-92). Shortly after, Soviet leader Leonid Brezhnev (1906-82) outlined what became known as the 'Brezhnev Doctrine' in a September issue of the newspaper *Pravda*:

> 'When forces that are hostile to socialism try to turn the development of some socialist country towards capitalism, it becomes not only a problem of the country concerned, but a common problem and concern of all socialist countries.'

As he said this, there was a build-up of Soviet forces along the borders that the USSR shared with China. In March 1969, there were skirmishes involving troops of the two countries on the uninhabited Damansky Island on the Ussuri River that marked the boundary between Manchuria and the USSR's Primorsky Krai (Maritime Provinces) in the far east of the country. The next few months would see further serious clashes in other regions close to the border. In this tense atmosphere, Chinese leader, Mao Zedong, saw an opportunity to isolate the Russians by making overtures towards the United States, a country that until then he would have no truck with.

The machinations to get Nixon and Mao together were complex, to say the least. The first real breakthrough came with the visit of a United States table tennis team in April 1971, the visit giving rise to the term 'ping-pong diplomacy' to describe the delicate manoeuvring that was going on. Following a series of secret visits by Kissinger to Beijing, where he held meetings with Chinese premier Zhou Enlai (1898-1976), an announcement was made that Nixon would visit China the following year. He arrived for the week-long visit on 21 February 1972, and he and his most senior advisers engaged in meetings with senior officials of the People's Republic of China. He also met Chairman Mao Zedong. In all of these meetings, Vietnam featured high on the agenda. The Chinese, initially hoping that the United States would be weakened by the drain on its resources the war represented, now feared that American weakness would only serve to make the USSR a stronger player on the world stage. The Chinese position had turned full circle and they were now eager to see a rapid end to the conflict. At the same time, of course, they wished to achieve this without losing their influence in communist North Vietnam, which might force Hanoi to turn to the Russians for help. For their part, the Russians rather liked the idea of having an ally on the southern Chinese border.

Meanwhile, Hanoi was extremely dismayed by China's rapprochement with America, recalling how the Chinese had let them down at the 1954 Geneva Conference and they objected to being discussed by the two superpowers without being present. In fact, the Chinese had advised North Vietnam some months earlier to put aside their objection to Thieu, so that a quick settlement could be arrived at and the Americans would leave Vietnam. Hanoi interpreted this request as an indication that Beijing wanted them to give up on their struggle to unify North and South Vietnam. The Shanghai Communiqué that was published at the conclusion of Nixon's visit to China seemed to confirm the North Vietnamese suspicion of Chinese motives. President Nixon committed to acknowledging but, importantly, not endorsing the People's Republic of China's One-China Policy with regard to Taiwan, the Republic of China – that there is only one state that should be called 'China'. Significantly, however, he also agreed to reduce the number of military installations on Taiwan 'as the tension in the area diminishes'. To Hanoi the only way that the tension in the region could be diminished was by an American withdrawal from Vietnam. The North Vietnamese felt as if they were being delivered a *fait accompli*. In spite of this, the Chinese were still keeping up with the Soviet Union in equipping North Vietnam to fight the war. Zhou Enlai had said that 'so long as the Vietnamese, the Laos, and Cambodians continue to fight, we will not stop supporting them for a single day.'

These supplies were going towards a build-up for another big push. In late 1971, convoys of lorries were spotted on the Ho Chi Minh Trail and the North Vietnamese were massing to the north of the Demilitarized Zone. Hanoi was hoping to exert pressure on America again in the year of a presidential election, with the campaign just beginning. But they also had something to prove to their allies, the Soviet Union and China. They had to know that the PAVN was capable of making effective use of all the equipment with which it was being supplied. The push was also aimed at convincing the United States, with a resounding victory, that Vietnamisation was futile and the only way out was through agreeing a settlement in Paris.

The Easter Offensive

What became known as the Easter Offensive in the West and the Nguyen Hue Offensive to the North Vietnamese began on 30 March with attacks by 120,000 communist troops and thousands of Viet Cong, attacking in three waves. They targeted provincial capitals and ARVN bases in the north, in the Central Highlands and along the Cambodian border to the north of Saigon. The Americans and South Vietnamese were caught on the hop and in Washington there was stunned horror, especially as just a few weeks previously, Secretary of Defense Laird had assured members of Congress that there was no serious possibility of attacks by the North Vietnamese and Viet Cong. Once it had started, there was a belief that it would not last. General Westmoreland, for instance, said that it would peter out 'in a matter of days'. He added, 'The staying power of the enemy is not great.' This was a complete miscalculation and the fighting – often furious – lasted until June, with both sides incurring significant casualties. B-52s were amongst the planes used in airstrikes against the North Vietnamese.

Back in Washington, the President was furious, both with Hanoi and, of course, with the Chinese and the Russians who had failed on this occasion to rein in the North Vietnamese. Behind it all, of course, was his fear of losing the forthcoming election. To defeat the communist action, prevent the complete collapse of the ARVN and to maintain US prestige during a forthcoming meeting with Soviet President Leonid Brezhnev, Nixon ordered a massive escalation. He authorised Operation Linebacker with the objective of disrupting the North Vietnamese supply chain and slowing the transportation of men and supplies. It would be the first continuous bombing initiative since President Johnson had called a halt to bombing in November 1968. The American forces in South Vietnam were, by this time seriously depleted. Of the 70,000 Americans still in the country, there were now only around 6,000 US combat troops and it was planned to ship most of those back to America within the next six months. Aerial strength was also lacking and had to be built up rapidly once the go-ahead for the operation had been given. Tactical strikes against North Vietnam – given the name 'Freedom Train' – were authorised on 5 April. On 10 April, 12 B-52s supported by 53 attack aircraft bombed petrol storage facilities around the town of Vinh.

By now, Nixon had decided to expand the bombing campaign and attack Hanoi and the port of Haiphong. This brought a risk that the Russo-US summit might be cancelled as Soviet ships offloaded their cargoes there. But, following Nixon's visit to China, the Kremlin had no intention of cancelling and letting Beijing gain the upper hand. American bombers destroyed bridges, roads, oil tanks and railway marshalling yards, laser-guided bombs being introduced for the first time. The bombing would continue until 23 October.

Meanwhile, in June and July, ARVN forces counter-attacked and the PAVN and Viet Cong were forced to withdraw from some of their initial gains. The city of Quang Tri on the North Central Coast of South Vietnam, to the north of Hue, was re-captured by September but the communists made some territorial gains along the border with Cambodia. The South Vietnamese army was a million strong, around half of whom were regular soldiers while the remainder were local units of fighting men. Even that number of men was not enough and Thieu had to move battalions to other parts of the country from the Mekong Delta where the communists had not taken action. But, as soon as ARVN troops had vacated their posts in the Delta, the Viet Cong moved in, occupying more than 100 government bases in the region. The communists were looking ahead to the possibility of a settlement that would leave the two sides where they were. At that moment, the Provisional Revolutionary Government of the Republic of South Vietnam, the underground government established by the Viet Cong, wanted to be in control of as much of South Vietnam as possible.

There was stark evidence throughout the Easter Offensive of the failings of Vietnamisation. Although the ARVN performed relatively well, most of the decisions had been made by US military advisers who were often forced to seize command of ARVN units that would otherwise have been routed. The bombing was also a decisive factor in stopping the communists from bringing down the Saigon government. In the south alone, B-52s flew almost 5,000 sorties, dropping their loads on An Loc where there was ferocious fighting and in the area around Quang Tri. It was a salutary lesson for the politicians and strategists in Hanoi. United States air power was always going to be difficult to overcome and perhaps the North Vietnamese Army did not have what it would take to force a settlement out of the Americans. Meanwhile, Thieu watched with growing anxiety, knowing how exposed he would be if the Americans left. He could only imagine what would happen if Nixon and Kissinger were to reach a settlement with Hanoi that permitted North Vietnamese troops to remain in South Vietnam. Nixon was publicly optimistic about the ARVN performance during the offensive, but in private he was less so, noting in his diary thoughts that expressed the dilemma America had faced from the start of the war: 'The real problem, is that the enemy is willing to sacrifice in order to win,' he wrote, 'while the South Vietnamese simply aren't willing to pay that much of a price in order to avoid losing.'

Nixon Goes to Moscow

Nixon was due to meet Soviet leader Leonid Brezhnev in Moscow in the spring of 1972 when nuclear arms and Vietnam would be high on the agenda. Before the summit, Nixon wanted to adopt a strong approach on Vietnam, warning Brezhnev that if he did not persuade the North Vietnamese to accept a peace settlement, he would cancel the meeting. Kissinger, however, although advising a tough stance on Vietnam, cautioned the president to be more flexible. If the summit were cancelled there would be severe repercussions for the global balance of power. Anyway, Kissinger was not at all sure that the Kremlin enjoyed sufficient influence over Hanoi to achieve that. When Kissinger flew to Moscow to prepare for the summit, he appears to have made a major concession regarding Vietnam. It implied that 'mutual withdrawal' was no longer on the table. Kissinger later claimed that 'mutual withdrawal' had been dropped long before and that this concession was mentioned simply to keep the Soviets involved in the negotiations for a settlement. Naturally, Hanoi rejected the offer. They were hardly likely to withdraw their troops in the midst of a major offensive and they were also suspicious of the veracity of the offer.

When Kissinger returned from Moscow, he found a president increasingly preoccupied with Vietnam, almost to the exclusion of everything else. He accused Kissinger of being too focused on a negotiated settlement and worried that the North Vietnamese were, in fact, stalling on the peace negotiations in order to wait for the election in November so that they could settle with a Democratic Congress. Thus, he sent Kissinger to Paris again to 'settle or else'. He brought his 'lunatic' strategy into play once again but little changed and there was a real danger that the Kremlin might cancel the summit. Nixon, meanwhile, had decided to launch the bombing campaign as a response to the Easter Offensive but both Kissinger's and Nixon's fears about the Kremlin's reaction to the bombing were unfounded. They received little more than a mild rebuke. Vietnam, it seemed, would not be allowed by Moscow to get in the way of 'détente', as the de-stressing of relations between Washington and the Kremlin was being called.

In spite of everything that had happened, the Paris talks resumed on 1 August. In fact, it might have been because of everything that had happened that they returned to Paris, since neither of them had gained any great advantage at the negotiating table through the actions of the previous months. Thieu was still saying there would be no recognition of his North Vietnamese enemy, there would be no coalition with the North Vietnamese and there would be no surrender of South Vietnamese territory. But, it seemed to Kissinger as they began to talk that something had given in the North Vietnamese approach. No longer did it seem that they were linking the political and military issues, and the demand for Thieu's departure seemed no longer to be a prerequisite for a settlement. American intelligence in South Vietnam discovered that the communist cadres in the south were being warned to prepare for a settlement and, in a speech made by North Vietnamese Prime Minister Pham Van Dong, Thieu's name did not even come up.

The deadline Hanoi had set was 7 November, the date of the 1972 US presidential election. The Democratic candidate, George McGovern, had split his party and there was little chance of him winning. It was evident, therefore, that the North Vietnamese were going to have to put up with Nixon for the next four years. In October, Kissinger and Le Duc Tho discussed the terms of an agreement – a ceasefire, prisoner exchanges, Thieu's government to remain in place temporarily and the PAVN units in the south to remain there. In other words, the political questions would be left in the hands of the Republic of Vietnam and the Democratic Republic of Vietnam. A 'council of national reconciliation' would be formed, consisting of representatives of the Saigon government, the communists and what were termed 'neutral' representatives, tasked with organising elections and bringing stability to Vietnam. North Vietnam and South Vietnam would, meanwhile, continue to operate as different countries, their armies staying where they were when the agreement was signed. The United States seemed, in reality, to have made the greatest concessions, as all remaining US air and ground forces were to be withdrawn, the last US combat unit having flown home in August. The North Vietnamese approved the agreement on 21 October and on 26 October, Kissinger announced that 'peace was at hand'. But Nixon now decided to delay matters, believing that it would look bad to the electorate to abandon President Thieu and his government. He told the North Vietnamese that 'the difficulties in Saigon have proved somewhat more complex than originally anticipated'. He was of the opinion that Thieu, who was, of course, vehemently opposed to the agreement, would come round once he realised that Congress would in all likelihood cut off his aid when it re-convened in January.

Suddenly, on 24 October, the situation deteriorated when Thieu condemned the draft treaty and issued an order to the ARVN that the communists in the south were to be 'wiped out quickly and mercilessly'. Hanoi accused the United States of trying to wreck the proposed agreement but Kissinger, speaking at a press conference in an effort to reassure Hanoi of the United States' sincerity, announced that he still believed that an agreement was in sight. There were problems with this, however. Firstly, it raised expectations in America that peace was very close. Secondly, it irritated Richard Nixon who saw it as displaying weakness to the communists and thirdly, it gave Thieu another reason to be upset with the Americans. Nixon toned down the message, saying that there were 'differences that must be resolved'.

Nixon Re-elected

On 7 November, Richard Nixon was re-elected in a landslide victory over George McGovern who was hampered by a lack of support from his own party, the fact that he was something of an outsider in Washington and the perception of him as a left-wing extremist. He had adopted a policy of unilateral withdrawal from Vietnam, a position that Nixon's campaign was able to depict as being radical and even a threat to the security of the United States. A robbery at the Democratic headquarters in the Watergate Building in June that involved White House staff members did not even put a dent in Nixon's huge win. He gained 60.7 per cent of the vote and won 520 Electoral College votes against a mere 17 won by McGovern.

Just a few days after the election, the talks resumed, continuing into December with Nixon desperate for a resolution before his inauguration on 20 January. The Americans did everything they could to resolve the problem of Thieu, proposing restrictions on the activities of the PAVN while providing significant amounts of new equipment to the ARVN. Military advisers were guaranteed to Thieu even after all Americans had been withdrawn and Nixon assured him that, if the communists violated the agreement in any way, especially if they attacked ARVN forces, B-52 strikes would be ordered. Although unaware of these promises, Hanoi made a few new demands of its own. By the time the talks broke up for Christmas, on 13 December, Kissinger was at his wit's end, frustrated by both Hanoi and Saigon. A major problem, of course, was that the Americans no longer had any leverage. Their position was clear and simple – they wanted out. Kissinger told Nixon that they could either wait and resume the negotiations in January or they could do something drastic and persuasive such as launching a new bombing campaign to remind the DRV of American firepower and let them know that the United States would not be pushed around. Nixon issued an ultimatum to Hanoi on 14 December, warning them that if they did not begin talking 'seriously' within 72 hours, there would be repercussions. He ordered the Joint Chiefs of Staff to prepare massive air strikes, lifting restrictions that had been imposed on such strikes for years, much to the chagrin of the generals who had always bemoaned such limitations. 'I don't want any more of this crap about the fact that we couldn't hit this target or that one,' Nixon told Admiral Thomas Moorer (1912-2004), head of the JCS, 'This is your chance to use military power to win this war, and if you don't, I'll hold you responsible.' Operation Linebacker II, or the 'Christmas Bombing' as it became known in the media, was launched on 18 December. It was the most intensive bombing campaign of the entire war, and the largest heavy bomber strikes by the United States since the Second World War, with 40,000 tons of bombs being dropped within a heavily-populated sixty-mile long stretch of North Vietnam between Hanoi and Haiphong. In eleven days until 29 December, B-52s flew around 3,000 sorties. The operation was controversial then and remains so today, the American media reacting with outrage, calling it 'savage and senseless' and 'Stone Age barbarism'. Reaction abroad was no less excoriating. Swedish Prime Minister Olof Palme (1927-86) compared the bombings to war crimes such as the bombing of Guernica, the Sharpeville massacre and the extermination of Jews and other groups at Treblinka. 'Now another name can be added to this list,' he said, 'Hanoi, Christmas 1972.' Nixon was unmoved. A guest at a White House dinner on the first night of the bombing said that the president 'did not care if the whole world thought he was crazy... if it did, so much the better, the Russians and Chinese might think they were dealing with a madman and so had better force North Vietnam into a settlement before the world was consumed in a larger war.'

On 26 December, the North Vietnamese signalled their willingness to resume the talks when the bombing ended and on 8 January, Kissinger and Le Duc Tho met again in Paris. By the following day, the outstanding issues had been resolved to each side's satisfaction. Coincidentally, it was President Nixon's 60th birthday and the settlement was the best possible present. He had already contacted Nguyen Van Thieu with an ultimatum: 'You must decide now whether you desire to continue our alliance or whether you want me to seek a settlement with the enemy which serves US interests alone.' It was the end of the line for the South Vietnamese president who had been in office now for seven years. He had no option but to accept the settlement.

Many claimed that agreement was reached because America had finally used its full firepower in Operation Linebacker II. They argued that, had it been used earlier in the conflict, it would have been over years previously. It is hard to prove the truth of this line of thinking, however, because the North Vietnamese had already agreed to return to the negotiations in Paris before the bombing began. Additionally, as ever, they had weathered the '12 days of Dien Bien Phu in the air' as they called the bombing campaign and had inflicted considerable damage on the Americans. 27 US planes, including 15 B-52s, were shot down by North Vietnamese missiles, anti-aircraft guns and Russian-built MiG fighters. They lost 92 pilots and crew, 43 of whom died and 49 of whom were captured.

The Agreement on Ending the War and Restoring Peace in Vietnam, known as the Paris Peace Accords, was signed on 27 January 1973. 'We have finally achieved peace with honor,' Nixon announced triumphantly. The agreement, however, did not differ greatly from what had been on the table just a few months previously in October. Ultimately, it appeared, there had really been little point in Linebacker II. The only conceivable purpose it served was to reassure Thieu that America meant business and to give the North Vietnamese a taste of what they would face should the agreement not hold. But, what did it really achieve? The fighting stopped, of course, but there was still no political solution. Thieu remained in power in Saigon and DRV troops held large parts of South Vietnam and they were not going away. Forces were authorised by the agreement to remain wherever they were when it was signed, unlike in 1954 when the troops of the north were ordered back over the DMZ. One did not have to be a genius to recognise the danger such a situation represented. It was inevitable that there would be further conflict at some point. This time, however, there would be no American involvement.

POWs, Disengagement and Impeachment

Since 1961, almost 9,000 planes and helicopters had been lost in North and South Vietnam, Laos and Cambodia. Of the 3,000 crew lost, 2,000 had died and 1,000 were missing in action. There were around 600 US military personnel in captivity. The Peace Accords allowed for the exchange of prisoners of war, the first 115 Americans being freed on 12 February 1973. The 24,000 US troops still in Vietnam when the peace agreement was signed were withdrawn at 15-day intervals to fit in with a series of prisoner releases by Hanoi. By the end of March, 591 POWs had been freed and flown home. Many had been held in the infamous 'Hanoi Hilton' prison as well as other prisons where they had been treated not as prisoners of war in accordance with the Geneva Convention but as war criminals who had committed 'crimes against humanity' through the bombing of North Vietnam. These men were often tortured or kept in solitary confinement for long spells. Bad treatment was meted out, especially to those who refused to broadcast anti-war statements or who refused to cooperate. Their release permitted a modicum of celebration in the United States at the military bases into which they flew and in the towns that welcomed them back and many attended a White House banquet thrown by President Nixon. This was in contrast to the welcome home that tens of thousands of ordinary soldiers received. There were no parades or celebrations for them and many felt that the country was ashamed of them. South Vietnamese prisoners were also treated savagely but it was not just the North Vietnamese who abused their captives. The South Vietnamese could be equally cruel towards their Viet Cong captives. Meanwhile, President Thieu was not averse to locking up critics of his own regime and many languished in South Vietnam's overcrowded jails. The Communists, too, were intolerant of criticism and many dissidents were also incarcerated.

Only when the last POW landed on American soil could Nixon at last relax in the knowledge that American involvement in Indochina was finally at an end. In April 1969 there had been 543,000 American military personnel in Vietnam; by April 1973, there were just 209, stationed at the US embassy in Saigon.

Nixon had intimated that the United States was still prepared to intervene in Vietnam if the North Vietnamese breached the terms of the Peace Accords, but on 4 June 1973 a bill was passed in Congress that blocked funds for future US military operations in Indochina. Nixon and Kissinger worked frantically to delay the ban's introduction until 15 August so that bombing could continue in Cambodia which had not been included in the peace agreement.

Other matters began to occupy President Nixon, however, as the Watergate scandal began to engulf his presidency. His special counsel, John Dean, made accusations of illegalities committed by the White House and a Nixon aide, Alexander Butterfield (born 1926), revealed the existence of tape recordings of conversations in the Oval Office that would back up Dean's accusations. The president was fatally wounded and Congress began to take control of foreign policy, Indochina featuring very low on its list of priorities. Meanwhile, although Kissinger believed Hanoi to be adding to the number of its troops in the south, the CIA estimated that there were approximately 150,000 North Vietnamese troops in South Vietnam, roughly the same number as the previous year. In any event, there seemed little hope for the Thieu government.

8

The Fall of South Vietnam
1973 to 1975

Vietnamese Fight Vietnamese

Of course, Vietnamese had fought Vietnamese over the centuries but the recent conflict had been part of a global struggle over competing ideologies – communism and capitalism. The Americans had departed the battlefield, but the fighting would continue, each side still benefitting from aid from their partners. The Saigon government claimed that it was in control of 75 per cent of the land and 85 per cent of the population of South Vietnam but in many areas the government was unpopular and the people's sympathies lay more with the National Liberation Front than with Thieu's corrupt regime. His troops urgently tried to secure any disputed territory as soon as the ink was dry on the Peace Accords, Thieu spreading his forces thinly across the country and trying to establish control over as much territory as he could. But this made them increasingly vulnerable to attack by the PAVN which was also benefitting from a black market in American-supplied military equipment. The North Vietnamese forces in the south had been weakened by the Easter Offensive and the bombing of Operation Linebacker II and were in need of supplies and men, forcing them to avoid confrontation with their enemy so that they could reestablish their strength. However, in 1973 the Ho Chi Minh Trail was busy once again as a huge quantity of equipment and around 100,000 men were transported along it. They constructed roads in the south, built pipelines and increased their political control of the areas where they were strong. Contrary to what he had promised Thieu, Nixon took little action to prevent Hanoi from bolstering its forces. He had covertly promised North Vietnam reconstruction aid and tried to use that to slow down the re-supply of the PAVN in the south. He could also have resumed the bombing of the supply routes but was reluctant to jeopardise the POW release programme. Meanwhile, the economy of South Vietnam was in deep trouble following the Americans' departure and inflation was rife. The huge American bases had provided employment for many and those jobs were now gone. The problems were not helped by the large numbers of refugees.

When the POWs had finally all been repatriated, Nixon and Kissinger began to consider the bombing of North Vietnam's supply routes. Naturally, they were aware of the probable public outrage at such a step, but Hanoi was blatantly violating the agreement. Now into his second term, Nixon believed that he had nothing to lose in recommencing the aerial attacks but, before he could do so, his presidency imploded. On 23 March 1973, the seven men who had been convicted of the break-in at the Watergate building were due to be sentenced by Judge John Sirica (1904-92). The likelihood of a long term of imprisonment led one of them, James McCord (born 1924), to write to Sirica, in the hope of receiving more lenient treatment. His letter alleged that perjury had been committed and that the defendants had been pressured into remaining silent. He indicated that others had been involved and they had connections to the Nixon White House. Sirica persuaded other defendants to talk and the trail led back to Special Counsel John Dean (born 1938) and Attorney General John Mitchell (1913-88). Gradually, the web of illegal activity that had been covered up began to be exposed to a stunned American public and for the next eighteen months, the Nixon administration was embroiled in hearings and trials, leading both Nixon and Kissinger to claim these diversions as the reason that they were unable to enforce the Paris Peace Accords. The blame for the eventual downfall of South Vietnam was ascribed by them to a Congress that cut off support for the Thieu government and critics who used Watergate to bring down the president. And, indeed, aid was being cut off. Around $3 billion was required to maintain the ARVN at a good standard, but that had already been cut and the fiscal year of 1973/74 would see a drastic reduction in the budget to around $1.1 billion. Funding for the bombing of Cambodia was cut off by Congress on 10 May 1973 and America now had nothing with which to beat the North Vietnamese. Another bill later in the year stopped any money going towards the re-building of North Vietnam while Hanoi refused to account for the many Americans missing in action. Then, on 7 November, the War Powers Resolution was passed by Congress. It stipulated that a president could not commit the United States to armed conflict without Congressional consent. It was a demonstration, if one were needed, of the disapproval felt by the nation's legislators about the manner in which Nixon and his predecessors had gone about the war in Vietnam and required the president to notify Congress of the deployment of US forces into actual or possible combat abroad within 48 hours. Furthermore, without a formal declaration of war or other Congressional authorisation to continue the deployment, it had to be ended within sixty days.

All of this gave Nixon and Kissinger grounds to blame Congress for the failure of South Vietnam to survive. The budgetary and other restrictions placed on helping the country were what allowed Hanoi to ride roughshod over the ceasefire by resupplying those in the south and it also enabled them to send more troops south without any fear of retribution from the United States. It seems evident, however, that Nixon did not have any real plan for the long-term survival of South Vietnam after the withdrawal of US forces. It was mostly about Nixon's own standing at home and the credibility of the United States as a global power. It was for that reason that Nixon tried to ensure there was a period of calm in Vietnam so that he could persuade people that he had, indeed, won an honourable peace by standing firm against Hanoi.

Meanwhile, the first six months of 1973 were frenzied as investigative journalists did their best to uncover presidential involvement in illegal acts. The existence of the tape recordings from the Oval Office was revealed in July and it seemed that at last some proof would be found to back up John Dean's testimony. Their existence was one thing, however; actually getting to listen to them was another and it took months of legal manoeuvring before the US Supreme Court ordered Nixon to release them. While this was going on, Vice President Spiro Agnew became only the second US Vice President to resign from office. He had pleaded no contest to charges of tax evasion as part of the resolution to a case where he was accused of accepting bribes during his time as Governor of Maryland. He was fined $10,000 and put on three years' probation. He eventually had to hand over $268,482 – the exact amount he had taken in bribes – to the Maryland State Treasurer in 1983. House Minority Leader Gerald Ford (1913-2006) took over the position of Vice President but his tenure was brief. On 1 August 1974, he was informed that clear evidence had been found that Nixon had committed a felony when he gave orders for the CIA to interfere with the FBI's investigation of the break-in at the Watergate Building. Nixon would have to resign or he would be impeached. On 9 August 1974, he resigned – the only US president to do so – and was replaced as President of the United States by Gerald Ford. Nixon's cohort, Kissinger, was retained as national security adviser and secretary of state.

President Ford Takes Office

Ford had been hawkish regarding Vietnam, supporting the actions of Kennedy and Johnson in sending troops in. As House Minority Leader, he had, however, criticised Johnson, complaining that he could see no justification in sending more troops to Vietnam while the White House prohibited air strikes on supply lines and industrial facilities in North Vietnam. 'Why are we pulling our best punches in Vietnam?' he asked. One of Nixon's last acts as president was to sign and bring into law a bill that set a cap of $1 billion on aid to South Vietnam for the next eleven months. Several days after he had vacated the White House, the House of Representatives cut another $300 million off that amount. Ford hastily wrote to President Thieu to reassure him of America's continued support, although he did not find out until months later about Nixon's promise to the South Vietnamese president that America would respond to any violation by Hanoi of the peace agreement with 'full force'. But some, including US Ambassador to the Republic of Vietnam, Graham Martin (1912-90), blamed such cuts for the inevitable fall of South Vietnam. The South Vietnamese Ambassador to the United States, Bui Diem, believed the steps being taken by Congress were an affront to the dignity and standing of a great nation. No consideration was being given to the 20 million Vietnamese, he argued, and even though Americans were no longer dying in Vietnam, they would not even give sufficient aid for the Republic of Vietnam to defend itself against the communists.

Indeed, the cuts began to have a real impact on the ARVN which was forced into what was described at the time as 'a poor man's war'. Hanoi had been fearful that the USA would at some point re-enter the war but, as time passed, this became increasingly unlikely until it reached the point where, even if they did, they would be unable to alter the likely outcome of a North Vietnamese victory and the fall of the Republic of Vietnam. In mid-December, the communists attacked the provincial capital of Phuoc Long, anticipating reprisal American air strikes. There were none and no ARVN troops arrived to defend the town. A month later, Phuoc Long and the province of which it was capital were in communist hands. Hanoi now knew that the Americans really were out of the war. Prime Minister Pham

Van Dong reassured the Politburo in Hanoi of this fact when he told them, 'I'm kidding, but also telling the truth when I say that the Americans would not come back even if you offered them candy.' A major offensive was approved for spring 1975.

The Final Push

As Congress debated a request from the president for extra aid for South Vietnam and Cambodia on 10 March 1975, Hanoi launched its offensive with an attack on Buon Ma Thuot in the Central Highland region. Ironically, at the very moment that the town fell to the communists, the legislators on Capitol Hill were rejecting the request for increased aid. Thieu, alarmed at the speed with which the offensive was proceeding, was now faced with some difficult decisions. To truncate the area his troops had to defend, he withdrew his forces eastwards from the Central Highlands, attempting to deploy them more effectively in coastal areas where there was a greater concentration of population. This, of course, left large areas undefended and the North Vietnamese quickly gobbled them up. The strategically important towns of Pleiku and Kon Tum fell under communist control and the withdrawal of the South Vietnamese troops turned into a disaster. As ARVN commanders sent troops to the north to defend Hue and Da Nang, there was chaos. The people in the affected areas took to the coastal roads which became blocked by refugees as well as fleeing ARVN troops, all trying to make their way south. This made any cohesive military operation virtually impossible, a situation exacerbated by confusing orders and a lack of command. To make matters even worse, the ARVN faced a North Vietnamese force that was well-organised and hungry for victory. Most of the ARVN was destroyed as it fled eastwards and Hue and Da Nang had fallen by 30 March. With two-thirds of South Vietnam under communist control, a triumphant Hanoi unleashed the Ho Chi Minh Campaign with the objective of liberating Saigon and the rest of South Vietnam from the Thieu government. On 10 April, as the remnants of the ARVN re-grouped around the capital, awaiting the inevitable, President Ford requested close to a billion dollars in military and economic aid for South Vietnam to help him, as he put it 'keep America's word good throughout the world.' The request was denied, probably on the grounds that it seemed obvious that no amount of money could make any difference in Vietnam.

As the PAVN moved inexorably towards Saigon, there were some moments of resistance. South Vietnamese troops fought valiantly at the key transportation hubs of Xuan Loc and Phan Rang, delaying the PAVN advance for several weeks until they were forced to withdraw on 22 April. With 100,000 troops now advancing on Saigon, the world waited for America's response. President Ford delivered it in a speech to students at Tulane University, making it clear that America was finished with Indochina and that the war should be consigned to history:

'Today, America can regain the sense of pride that existed before Vietnam. But it cannot be achieved by refighting a war that is finished as far as America is concerned. As I see it, the time has come to look forward to an agenda for the future, to unify, to bind up the Nation's wounds, and to restore its health and its optimistic self-confidence.'

Thieu finally buckled under extraordinary pressure on 21 April when he resigned, full of recriminations towards the United States, accusing it of breaking its promises and abandoning him and his country. He hoped that a new leader would emerge who would be more acceptable to Hanoi and the following day, General Duong Van Minh was sworn in as the last president of the Republic of Vietnam. Minh had been the leader of the 1963 coup that had ended the presidency of Ngo Dinh Diem and, until he had withdrawn, had been a candidate to replace Thieu in the 1971 election.

US ambassador Graham Martin irritated the Pentagon by refusing to order an evacuation of embassy staff, because he was worried about creating panic in Saigon, and that the South Vietnamese might turn on the Americans. By 28 April, it had become impossible to fly in and out of Saigon's Tan Son Nhat airport which had been hit by rockets and heavy artillery strikes. The following day, the ambassador finally gave the order for a helicopter evacuation to begin, an operation dubbed 'Frequent Wind'. The American radio station in Saigon began repeated playing of the song *White Christmas*, the signal for all US personnel to assemble at designated evacuation points. Buses moved through the city, collecting people and transporting them to a compound at the airport. By the evening, 395 Americans and more than 4,000 Vietnamese had been evacuated to ships in the South China Sea. However, there were still several thousand Americans and Vietnamese stranded at the embassy in Saigon. Meanwhile, outside the embassy, crowds of Vietnamese clamoured to gain entry to the compound and claim refugee status. In thunderstorms, the helicopter evacuation continued throughout that evening and night, plucking people off rooftops and providing some of the most dramatic footage of the entire war. At 3.45 the following morning, with Saigon about to fall at any time, the ambassador was given the order by President Ford and Henry Kissinger that only Americans were now to be evacuated. Ambassador Martin departed on a helicopter at 5 am by which time 978 Americans and around 1,100 Vietnamese had been airlifted out of the embassy compound. The last Marines guarding the embassy left at 7.53 am.

At 6 am on 29 April, Hanoi ordered General Van Tien Dung (1917-2002) to 'strike with the greatest determination straight into the enemy's final lair', and a day later, after a huge bombardment, the North Vietnamese were ready to advance into Saigon. It was soon obvious that the ARVN was not going to be able to mount much resistance. At 10.42 am, Minh announced an unconditional surrender, inviting the Provisional Revolutionary Government to join in 'a ceremony of orderly transfer of power so as to avoid any unnecessary bloodshed in the population.' His invitation was ignored by troops who had no interest in a peaceful transfer of power. Around noon, a T-54 tank of the People's Army of Vietnam crashed through the gates of the Independence Palace to find Minh waiting for them on the steps. He announced to Colonel Bui Tin (born 1927) that he had been waiting in order to transfer power to him, but Tin's reply was curt. 'There is no question of you transferring power,' he said, 'Your power has crumbled. You cannot give up what you do not have.' Later that afternoon, Minh announced the dissolution of the South Vietnamese government.

It has been estimated that up to 3.8 million people died violently in the Vietnam War, including 195,000-430,000 South Vietnamese civilians and 50,000-65,000 North Vietnamese civilians. 58,220 Americans died and 303,644 were wounded. The ARVN lost somewhere between 171,331 and 220,357 men and the United States Department of Defense has estimated that 950,765 communist troops died between 1965 and 1974. There were casualties in the neighbouring countries, too. Between 200,000 and 300,000 Cambodians lost their lives and around 60,000 Laotians.

Although the effects of the war would reverberate in Indochina for some time to come, and are still felt today, the warfare that had engulfed Vietnam for thirty years was at last over.

9

The Legacy of the Vietnam War

For the United States the Vietnam War left an indelible legacy. Its foreign policy would never be the same again and great caution would henceforth be exercised by US presidents and legislators in the deployment of US troops abroad. America, since the Vietnam War, has been more inclined to involve itself abroad only for short periods and to employ aerial bombing rather than send in troops in the way that happened in Vietnam. The desire to avoid 'another Vietnam' has become a leitmotif of US foreign policy in the last fifty years, the Iraq War being just one of the recent instances.

In 1984, in what became known as the Weinberger Doctrine, and with the lessons learned from Vietnam, US Secretary of Defense, Caspar Weinberger (1917-2006), delineated limits on future military intervention and the use of American forces abroad. He stipulated that they should be deployed when the vital national interests of the United States (or close allies) are threatened; war should be prosecuted wholeheartedly with the clear intention of winning; decisive force should be employed in the pursuit of clearly defined political and military objectives; the use of force will be continually reassessed to determine whether it is still necessary and appropriate; there must be a 'reasonable assurance' of Congressional and public support; and force should be used only as a last resort. The Gulf War of 1990 to 1991 is one example where all six of the above conditions were met. The Allied victory on that occasion supports the view that decisive strength might have provided America with a better outcome in Vietnam than what was achieved with a gradual escalation.

There had been around 125,000 draft-dodgers during the war, young men who had crossed the border into Canada to avoid being drafted and around 50,000 men deserted. In 1977, President Jimmy Carter granted unconditional pardon to all who had dodged the draft. The Vietnam War continues to cost the United States considerable sums of money; the government pays Vietnam veterans and their families in excess of $22 billion a year in claims related to the conflict.

Vietnam was largely isolated in the years following the end of the war. Until 1994, it was illegal for American companies to trade with it and the only help from the outside world came from the Soviet Union. But by the early 1990s there was an increasing rapprochement with the USA and diplomatic relations were established in 1995 during the administration of President Bill Clinton. Since then, Vietnam has not looked back economically.

The war is never far from the thoughts of the Vietnamese, particularly in view of the devastating effect it had on the landscape of the country. Bomb craters are still visible and the chemical deforestation of large areas of the country by the Americans has severely damaged the countryside. These chemicals are still having an effect, changing the landscape, causing illness and birth defects and poisoning the food chain. They have also affected the children of US veterans. The daily threat of thousands of undiscovered landmines remains even now.

Meanings of Common Acronyms
Used in the War

AATTV	Australian Army Training Team Vietnam
ANZUS	Australia, New Zealand, United States Treaty
ARVN	Army of the Republic of Vietnam
CEFEO	Corps Expéditionnaire Français en Extrême-Orient (French Far East Expeditionary Force)
CORDS	Civilian Operations and Revolutionary Development Support
COSVN	Central Office for South Vietnam (North Vietnamese/ NLF headquarters in Cambodia)
DESOTO	De Haven Special Operations off Tsingtao
DMZ	Demilitarised Zone
DRV	Democratic Republic of Vietnam
JCS	Joint Chief of Staff
MAAG	Military Assistance Advisory Group
MACV	Military Assistance Command Vietnam
NATO	North Atlantic Treaty Organisation
NLF	National Liberation Front for South Vietnam
NVA	North Vietnamese Army
OSS	Office of Strategic Services
PAVN	People's Army of Vietnam
RAN	Royal Australian Navy
SAM	Surface-to-Air Missile
SDS	Students for a Democratic Society

MEANINGS OF ACRONYMS

SEATO	Southeast Asia Treaty Organisation
VC	Viet Cong
VVAW	Vietnam Veterans Against the War

Bibliography and Filmography

It would be impossible to list all the books and films about the Vietnam War. Listed below are just a few:

Books about the Vietnam War

Histories

Karnow, Stanley, *Vietnam: A History*, New York: Viking, 1992

Lawrence, Mark Atwood, *The Vietnam War: A Concise International History*, New York: Oxford University Press, 2010

Prados, John, *Vietnam: The History of an Unwinnable War, 1945-1975 (Modern War Studies)*, Lawrence: University Press of Kansas, 2013

Schandler, Herbert Y., *America in Vietnam: The War That Couldn't Be Won*, Lanham: Rowman & Littlefield, 2011

Woodruff, Mark W., *Unheralded Victory: Who Won the Vietnam War?*, London: HarperCollins, 1999

Young, Marilyn, *Vietnam Wars, 1945-1990*, New York: Harper-Perennial, 1991

Novels and Memoirs

Bao Ninh, *The Sorrow of War*, London: Vintage, 1994

Caputo, Philip, *A Rumor of War*, London: Pimlico, 1999

Herr, Michael, *Dispatches*, London: Picador, 1991

Marlantes, Karl, *Matterhorn*, Corvus: London, 2011

Mason, Robert, *Chickenhawk*, London: Corgi, 1984
O'Brien, Tim, *If I Die In a Combat Zone*, London: Picador, 1991
Webb, James H., *Fields of Fire*, Bantam USA: New York, 2001

Films about the Vietnam War

Apocalypse Now, 1979, dir. Francis Ford Coppola
Born on the Fourth of July, 1989, dir. Oliver Stone
Casualties of War, 1989, dir. Brian de Palma
Full Metal Jacket, 1987, dir. Stanley Kubrick
Platoon, 1986, dir. Oliver Stone
The Deer Hunter, 1978, dir. Michael Cimino

Index

A Shau Valley, 76, 99, 100

Abrams, General Creighton, 84, 85, 100, 105, 106, 116

Acheson, Dean, 64, 81

Allen, George, 64

anti-war, 65, 66, 67, 68, 82, 84, 88, 89, 90, 103, 115, 122

Ap Bac, 41

Army of the Republic of Vietnam (ARVN), 37, 40, 41, 42, 44, 49, 54, 60, 65, 70, 72, 75, 76, 77, 79, 84, 97, 98, 99, 100, 104, 105, 107, 115, 116, 117, 119, 123, 128, 129, 130, 132, 133, 141, 143, 144, 145, 146, 147, 150

August Revolution, 21

Australia, 33, 44, 45, 46, 150

Australia, New Zealand, United States Treaty (ANZUS), 44, 46, 150

B-52, bomber, 57, 60, 96, 128, 129, 133, 134, 135

Ball, George, 40, 53, 54, 63

Bao Dai, Emperor, 21, 22, 26, 34, 35, 36

Binh Ba, Battle of, 46

Bowles, Chester, 41

Brezhnev, Leonid, 51, 125, 128, 130

Britain, 20, 32, 33, 58

Buddhist, 35, 42, 52, 65, 66, 76

Bundy, McGeorge, 63

Bundy, William, 54, 64

Bush, President George HW, 10

Cabot Lodge, Henry, 42, 49, 64

Calley, Lieutenant William, 112, 113

Cambodia, 16, 22, 33, 78, 95, 96, 97 104, 105, 106, 107, 108, 109, 110, 114, 115, 116, 127, 129, 136, 137 141, 144, 147 capitalism, 9, 29, 125, 139

Carter, President Jimmy, 10, 149

Carver, George, 81

Catholics, 15, 35, 42, 52

Cedar Falls, Operation, 60

China, 9, 17, 18, 19, 20, 25, 28, 29, 30, 45, 50, 53, 61, 62, 91, 94, 102, 123, 125, 126, 127, 128

Churchill, Sir Winston, 32

Civilian Operations and Revolutionary Development Support (CORDS), 62, 85, 105, 150

Clifford, Clark, 63, 64, 78, 80, 83, 120

Cochinchina, 15, 16, 22, 23

Collins, General J Lawton 'Lightning Joe', 34, 35, 37

Colson, Charles, 110, 122

communism, 9, 17, 25, 29, 30, 39, 43, 44, 47, 48, 80, 139

Coral-Balmoral, Battle of, 46

Corps Expéditionnaire Français en Extrême-Orient (French Far East Expeditionary Force – CEFEO), 22, 150

Cronkite, Walter, 73, 74, 83

d'Argenlieu, Admiral Thierry, 23

Da Nang, 11, 15, 54, 58, 70, 144

Dai Do, Battle of, 75

de Lattre de Tassigny, General Jean, 27

Demilitarised Zone (DMZ) 32, 75, 82, 127, 136, 150

Democratic Republic of Vietnam (DRV), 19, 21, 22, 25, 27, 28, 29, 31, 32, 33, 34, 41, 48, 54, 57, 58, 61, 94, 97, 114, 132, 134, 136, 150

Dewey Canyon III, 119, 121

Diem, Ngo Dinh, 21, 27, 31, 33, 34, 35, 36, 37, 38, 40, 42, 43, 44, 49, 54, 121, 122, 145

Dien Bien Phu, 9, 28, 32, 33, 34, 135

domino theory, 29, 31, 32, 39, 90

Dong Ha, 75, 76

doves, 68, 80

Duck Hook, Operation, 101, 102

Dulles, John Foster, 33, 35

Duong, General Van 'Big' Minh, , 49, 123, 145

Durbrow, Elbridge, 37

Easter Offensive, 127, 129, 131, 139

Eisenhower, President Dwight
    D, 28, 30, 31, 32, 33, 34, 37,
    39, 43, 90, 93
Ellsberg, Daniel, 120, 121, 122

Ford, President Gerald R, 48,
    142, 143, 145, 146,
France, 9, 10, 14, 15, 19, 20,
    21, 23, 24, 26, 27, 28, 29,
    30, 31, 32, 33, 30, 35, 36
Fulbright, J William, (hearings),
    67, 119

Geneva Agreement, 31-33, 36,
    50
Giap, General Vo Nguyen, 19,
    21, 24, 26, 27, 28, 69, 103
Ginsberg, Allen, 68
Goldwater, Barry, 52,
Great Society, 48, 55, 58, 67,
    80, 86, 88
Gulf of Tonkin Resolution, 52,
    55, 108

Habib, Philip, 81
Haiphong, 23, 25, 27, 128, 134
Haldeman, HR, 93, 94
Hamburger Hill (Hill 937), 100
Hanoi, 14, 16, 21, 25, 26, 27,
    35, 38, 50, 52, 53, 54, 56,
    59, 60, 61, 62, 63, 64, 68,
    69, 70, 71, 83, 84, 91, 97,
    102, 103, 105, 108, 115,
    116, 123, 124, 126, 127, 128,
    129, 130, 131, 132, 133, 134,
    136, 138, 140, 141, 142, 143,
    144, 145, 146
Harriman, W Averell, 41, 82,
    83, 91
hawks, 68, 80
Ho Chi Minh, 15, 17, 18, 19,
    21, 22, 23, 25, 28, 29, 31,
    33, 34, 35, 36, 37, 38, 40,
    52, 56, 59, 60, 62, 63, 68,
    69, 70, 75, 94, 05, 97, 101,
    102, 103, 116, 117, 123, 127,
    139, 144
Ho Chi Minh Trail, 38, 40, 49,
    53, 54, 57, 59, 71, 75, 97,
    116, 117, 123, 127
Hoa Binh, 11, 26, 27
Hoffman, Abbie, 68
Hue, 12, 15, 16, 17, 18, 21, 72,
    76, 99, 129, 144
Humphrey, Hubert , 85, 87, 88,
    89, 91, 92

Ia Drang Valley, 57
Indochina, 9, 10, 16, 19, 20, 23,
    24, 25, 26, 28, 29, 30, 31,
    32, 34, 43, 67, 68, 74, 78,
    79, 88, 90, 137, 138, 145,
    147
Indochinese Communist Party,
    17

Japan, 17, 19, 20, 21

Johnson, President Lyndon B, 33, 40, 46, 48, 49, 50, 51, 52, 53, 54, 55, 56, 58, 59, 62, 63, 64, 67, 68, 69, 74, 77, 78, 79, 80, 81, 82, 83, 84, 85, 86, 88, 90, 91, 92, 95, 96, 98, 105, 107, 120, 121, 128, 142

Joint Chiefs of Staff (JCS), 54, 63, 77, 78, 106, 134, 150

Junction City, Operation, 60

Kennedy, President John F, 33, 39, 40, 41, 42, 46, 48, 49, 50, 82, 90, 126, 142

Kennedy, Robert, 82, 85, 86, 87, 88, 89, 120

Kent State University, 109, 111

Kerry, John, 119, 121

Khe San, 73

King, Dr Martin Luther, 65, 67, 86

Kissinger, Henry, 95, 96, 97, 102,108, 114, 115, 116, 117, 120, 121, 122, 123, 124, 125, 130, 131, 132, 133, 134, 135, 137, 138, 140, 141, 142, 146

Korea, 11, 29, 30, 32, 59, 60, 93

Korea, North, 76, 93

Korea, South, 29, 46

Laird, Melvin, 98, 102, 114, 127

Lam Son, Operation, 116, 117

Lansdale, Brigadier-General Edward G, 35, 37, 38

Laos, 16, 22, 27, 28, 33, 38, 47, 76, 78, 96, 115, 116, 118, 119, 123, 127, 136

Le Duan, 103

Le Duc Tho, 114, 123, 124, 132, 135

Leclerc, General Jacques, 22

LeMay, General Curtis, 89-90

Linebacker I, Operation, 128;

Linebacker II, Operation, 134, 135, 136, 139

Lon Nol, 106, 107

Long Tan, Battle of, 45

Maddox, USS, 50, 51

madman theory, 93, 101, 102, 135

Mao Zedong, 24, 61, 94, 125, 126

McCarthy, Eugene, 81, 82, 85, 86, 87, 88, 89

McCarthy, Joseph, 29

McGovern, George, 85, 89, 103, 115, 131, 133

McNamara, Robert, 41, 42, 50, 54, 55, 58, 59, 62, 63, 64, 67, 78, 80, 120

Meadlo, Private Paul, 112, 113

Medina, Captain Ernest, 112, 113

Mekong Valley, 14, 15, 41, 56, 62, 70, 71, 129

Midway Island, 98, 101

Military Assistance Advisory Group (MAAG), 30, 150

Military Assistance Command Vietnam (MACV), 41, 49, 57, 60, 62, 70, 72, 73, 76, 84, 85, 150

Muhammad Ali (Cassius Clay), 67

My Lai Massacre, 111, 113

National Liberation Front (NLF), 38, 39, 40, 41, 42, 49, 50, 59, 60, 65, 97, 105, 111, 112, 139, 150

National Mobilization Committee to End the War in Vietnam, 68, 89

Navarre, General Henri, 28

New York Times, 67, 79, 120, 121

New Zealand, 33, 44, 46, 150

Ngo Dinh Can, 36

Ngo Dinh Diem. *See* Diem, Ngo Dinh

Ngo Dinh Khoi, 34

Ngo Dinh Nhu, 36, 42, 43

Nguyen Ai Quoc (*later* Ho Chi Minh), 17

Nguyen Cao Ky, 54, 59

Nguyen Van Thieu, General, 54, 59, 69, 70, 71, 85, 91, 92, 97, 98, 99, 101, 102, 114, 115, 117, 118, 122, 123, 124, 126, 129, 131, 132, 133, 135, 136, 137, 138, 139, 140, 141, 143, 144, 145

Nixon, President Richard M, 33, 85, 90, 91, 92, 93, 94, 95, 96, 97, 98, 100, 101, 102, 103, 104, 105, 106, 107, 108, 109, 110, 113, 114, 115, 116, 118, 119, 120, 121, 122, 123, 124, 125, 126, 128, 130, 131, 132, 133, 134, 135, 137, 140, 141, 142, 143

OPLAN 34Alpha, Operation, 50

pacification, 47, 60, 62, 63, 64, 77, 85, 98

Paris Peace Accords, 135, 136, 137, 139, 140

Pathet Lao, 116

Pentagon Papers, 79, 120, 121, 122, 146

People's Army of Vietnam (PAVN), 19, 24, 26, 60, 61, 69, 70, 71, 73, 74, 75, 75, 76, 80, 100, 107, 117, 127, 129, 132, 133, 139, 140, 145, 146, 147, 150

Pham Van Dong 19, 23, 131

Phan Boi Chau, 17

Philippines, 28, 33, 47

Phuoc Long, 143

Phuoc Tuy, 45, 46

Pleiku, 53, 57, 70, 144

Prisoners of War (POWs), 123, 136, 140

Provisional Revolutionary Government of the Republic of South Vietnam, 129, 147

Reagan, President Ronald, 10

Red River Valley, 11, 12, 25

Rogers, William, 102, 114

Rolling Thunder, 53, 58, 61, 96

Roosevelt, President Franklin D, 29, 48

Rostow, Walt, 40, 50, 63, 64

Rubin, Jerry, 68

Rusk, Dean, 50, 63, 120

Saigon, 10, 22, 26, 34, 35, 36, 40, 41, 42, 45, 49, 53, 54, 56, 65, 66, 69, 70, 71, 72, 75, 76, 77, 84, 85, 98, 99, 114, 118, 122, 123, 124, 127, 129, 132, 133, 136, 137, 139, 144, 145, 146

Sainteny, Jean, 22, 23

Sharp Jr, Admiral US Grant, 58

Sihanouk, Prince Norodom, 106

Silent Majority, 103, 104

Sirica, Judge John, 140

Southeast Asia Treaty Organisation (SEATO), 33, 36, 44, 151

Soviet Union, 19, 25, 28, 29, 32, 53, 61, 62, 91, 94, 95, 97, 102, 123, 125, 127, 149

Spock, Dr Benjamin, 66

State of Vietnam, 26, 30, 33, 34

Sudents for a Democratic Society (SDS), 66, 89, 150

Taiwan, 47, 126

Taylor, General Maxwell, 40, 42, 63

Tet Offensive, 45, 69, 70, 72, 74, 75, 77, 80, 84, 85, 111

Thailand, 33, 47, 53

Thieu, General Nguyen Van. See Nguyen Van Thieu, General

Thompson, Warrant Officer Hugh, 112, 113

Ticonderoga, USS, 51

Tonkin, Gulf incident, 27, 28, 50, 53, 55, 61, 108

Truman, President Harry S, 25, 29, 30, 31, 48, 81,

Turner Joy, USS, 51

Viet Cong, 13, 40, 41, 45, 53, 54, 60, 62, 65, 67, 69, 70,

71, 72, 73, 74, 75, 84, 85, 91, 96, 98, 105, 106, 112, 113, 117, 124, 127, 129, 137, 151

Viet Minh, 9, 19, 20, 21, 22, 23, 24, 25, 26, 27, 28, 32, 33, 34, 38

Viet Nam Doc Lap Dong Minh, 19 Vietnam Veterans Against the War (VVAW), 65, 119, 121, 149, 151

Vietnamisation, 97, 98, 99, 101, 104, 105, 116, 118, 123, 127, 129

Wallace, George, 89, 91
War Powers Resolution, 141
Watergate, 97, 121, 122, 133, 137, 140, 141, 142

Weinberger, Caspar (the Weinberger Doctrine), 148

Westmoreland, General William C, 49, 54, 55, 56, 57, 58, 59, 60, 62, 63, 65, 69, 70, 71, 72, 77, 78, 79, 84, 97, 113, 127

Wheeler, General Earle, 77, 78, 79, 81

Wise Men, 63, 64, 81

Wilson, Harold, 62

Wilson, President Woodrow, 18

Xuan Thuy, 83, 114

Youth International Party (Yippies), 87, 89

Zhou Enlai, 61, 125, 127